THE CUSTOM TOUCH
Creative Sewing Techniques

Mary J. Wadlington

Illustrations and Diagrams by the Author

Gem Publications
P.O. Box 2499
Melbourne, Florida 32901

Library of Congress Cataloging in Publication Data

Wadlington, Mary J., 1925-
    The custom touch.

1. Dressmaking — Pattern design. I. Title.
TT520.W14   646.4'304   81-13498
ISBN 0-941832-00-7   AACR2

ACKNOWLEDGEMENTS

In writing "The Custom Touch," it has been my privilege to have friends to encourage me and to offer helpful suggestions. I sincerely thank all of you.

A special thanks goes to my husband, who challenged me to write this book. He was also my critic, which was needful. Thanks are also in order to Ruth Higgins, Sandy Sheldon and Lorraine Prieto, my proofreaders, who helped to smooth out the raw edges and offered so many helpful suggestions. Also, Alan Denis gave me valuable technical advice.

I also wish to express gratitude to all of my students who have, through the years, helped me to become more proficient as a teacher. Especially do I thank Sydna Ferguson who, many years ago, convinced me that the home-sewer does want to learn pattern-making, and organized my first class.

And to the One who is the source of my strength and vitality.

"A book should serve as the ax for the
frozen sea within us." . . . Franz Kafka

CONTENTS

CONTENTS

CONTENTS

CONTENTS

WHO, ME?

Lookout, Geoffrey Bean, Bill Blass, Albert Nippon, Sasson and all the rest of you great designers! Here comes the new breed, *the creative sewer!*

These days, it's back to doing things for yourself. And what more rewarding way than being your own designer and custom dress couturiere.

Who, Me? Yes, You! You can design and make your own patterns. If you can crochet, knit, embroider, macrame, or work puzzles, you can design and make your own patterns. With the *method of programmed learning* used in "The Custom Touch," you can progress from the very simplest patterns to the most difficult, without even realizing it, because the transition is so enjoyable. Then you can copy expensive designer clothes, or you can use your own ideas. Any way you choose, you will be well dressed. You know, so many times when you see a dress that you would like to copy, you can't find a commercial pattern to use to make it up. And commercial patterns are so expensive; you can really save money making your own. It doesn't take a lot of time with the easy step-by-step directions given in "The Custom Touch." Once you get the hang of it, you can make a dress pattern in fifteen minutes, and your own patterns are so much easier to work with than commercial patterns because all the pattern pieces fit together perfectly.

Not only does "The Custom Touch" give you pattern-making directions, it also gives sewing tips on the patterns and also covers such things as how to sew an almost invisible hem, how to interface properly, turn curves, sew points, and all those other things that can make the difference between a professional-looking garment and one that looks "home-made."

"The Custom Touch," for the first time, has, in clear, concise, simple terms, the directions for making your own basic form pattern, which is the guide you will use in making your patterns. This form pattern is made to fit the individual curves of your body. This means that every design that you make from this form pattern will fit.

So put something new, something different, into your sewing. Give your clothes that *custom touch* that comes from knowing how to create from the beginning. And while you're making your patterns, you'll be learning pattern concepts that will enlarge your sewing horizons. Sewing will be easier, faster, and more rewarding than you ever thought possible.

Now is the time for you to realize your full potential. Be creative and know the self-satisfaction of being your own dress designer.

PATTERN TALK

The objective of this book is to reach the home sewer who wants to perfect her sewing talent, but hasn't the time for a thorough study program. In writing in such simple terms, there is no intent to belittle, but to simply eliminate all complicated details that take valuable time to master. And yet, if you master the lessons in these pages, you will be able to create just about any type of clothing you want. The methods presented in "The Custom Touch" have been devised from many years of teaching pattern making to the home sewer.

Experience teaches us the simplest and easiest methods to obtain results. I was blessed with four daughters — Susan and the triplets, Jenny, Janice and Judy. What an experience! What fun designing and making dresses for four lovely daughters. You know how particular teenagers can be about their dress, so being able to create whatever they wanted was rewarding, as well as exacting.

Have you ever longed to copy an original design or to design a dress from your own ideas? Let me show you how to accomplish this in an exciting and rewarding way, by creating your own patterns. Pattern making can be delightful and the small amount of effort (much less than re-working a commercial pattern to fit) will be offset by the results of your accomplishment. And once you have accomplished pattern making, you will be a better seamstress because you understand why you handle a pattern cut as you do.

One step at a time is all you need to be concerned with. All unnecessary pattern ritual and jargon has been eliminated so that you, as a novice, can easily understand. I will try to communicate with you as if we were communicating in person. Remember, there is nothing mysterious about pattern making. It is just like learning any other kind of craft.

We will use the *Flat Pattern Method*, as it is the easiest and most versatile method of creating a design. To get a perspective of Flat Pattern designing, just imagine taking a flat piece of fabric and shaping to to fit the body. We know that we will have to fold it to fit the curves of the body. We call this *Figure Contour*. We control Figure Contour with *Dart Control*. Dart Control, which will be discussed continually throughout this book, is the main ingredient in pattern design. This will be elaborated on more fully as we progress through the lessons.

So come on. Let's take a journey into an exciting and creative area of sewing.

> "She selects wool and flax
>   and works with eager hands.
> When it snows, she has no fear
>   for her household:
> For all of them are clothed
>   in scarlet."   Proverbs

HIGH STYLE

"High Style" is the current new look or designs. There are some who say a woman should always wear what looks attractive on her regardless of current styles. Well, that may be, but you will usually look as if you have had-it-around for awhile, if it doesn't have any semblance to present trends. The solution is to check all of the latest styles and from those, choose what will be the most becoming to you.

No longer, however, can we designate certain designs to certain occasions. The good sense of modern women have allowed them to blend styles to achieve a tailored look with a feminine approach.

Solomon said, "There is nothing new under the sun." It's still true today. Styles change from year to year, but with almost certainty, styles repeat themselves every few years. At this writing, I'm witnessing much nostalgia every time I shop or look at a fashion magazine. All of the styles that I wore as a young woman are now the latest fashions. The blouson has been in style off and on repeatedly. Skirts go up and down. But, with all the style changes, you will be able to be well dressed and in "High Style" if you create your own wardrobe.

If you have design talent, which is being able to view a new look in your mind, great! You can really elaborate on the basic pattern cuts. If not, follow the latest trends. Make a scrapbook of styles that appeal to you. These can be from magazines and newspapers. You will be able to copy these designs or to blend ideas from several different designs.

The really exciting thing is that, once you have learned the basic pattern cuts, you will be able to create whatever current styles dictate along with your own style preferences. Every new style will catch your eye and you will want to work it up.

LOOK AND SEE

Start to observe. Learn to really "look and see." Notice details. Notice what's new. What are designers doing in the way of trims? What's IN? Maybe lace trim is the big thing, or is it piping, braid or rick-rack? Take Note! Also notice pockets, collar or sleeve changes. These occur more frequently than changes in the body portion of clothing. Notice colors. What color combinations are designers using?

And speaking of color, learn what your colors are. This is important. A dress will lose its appeal if the color is wrong for the wearer. To determine the right colors for you, use handkerchief-size swatches of fabric and stand in front of a mirror with the swatches against your face. What does each color do for your face? Does it light it up or does it look pale or ruddy? Stay away from colors that seem to blend with your skin. You should be able to see immediately what looks well on you. If you can't be objective, ask a friend to help you.

Carry a scratch pad in your pocketbook to sketch details of any design that you would like to work up.

After you begin to conscientiously "look and see," you will find that it is becoming second nature with you. Good luck!

PATTERN TALK

LET'S TALK ABOUT THE BASIC PATTERN

The Basic Pattern, which is a Flat Pattern, is used as a basis for all of the designs in this book. The basic pattern does not have seam allowances as these would be in the way of constructing the designs. The darts are also cut out. You will see the need for this later. Seams are added to the pattern in the final step. The Basic Pattern, of course, is a half pattern as is a commercial pattern.

This one pattern can be converted into any design simply by moving or changing darts or adding additional space to cover gathers, pleats, tucks or seams.

You can make your own Basic Pattern from the directions in the final chapter of this book. I hope you will, because this will be a superior fit. Many hours were spent perfecting this technique and I feel that it will be worth the time you will spend making it. And remember, you only have to make it once. If you wish, you may purchase a commercial basic pattern. Try to find one that fits your shoulders properly. You can regulate the rest of the pattern better than you can the shoulders. You will re-work this pattern to fit your body as closely as possible. There are a number of books written on this subject. After re-working, cut off the seam allowances and cut out the darts.

Your Basic Pattern should be made out of something sturdy, such as lightweight cardboard, heavy pellon or even oil cloth. You will transfer your self-made or commercial re-worked pattern to this heavier substance. This will allow you to store and keep it well. You see, you do not actually use the original pattern in making your designs, but only copies of it. To make copies, lay six pieces of newspaper together and pin carefully. Trace the original pattern onto this and cut out. Store for future use. You may prefer to use some other kind of paper, but I prefer newspapers. I often use the columns as a guide while constructing a design.

Although some designers use a bodice front pattern with only a waistline dart as a basis for working out designs, I prefer using the divided dart method which distributes the control more evenly. Also, with my method of making a basic pattern (described in the last chapter of this book) the side dart actually shapes the area between the armhole and bust. And, too, many of the designs need only the dart control from the side dart. You will be able to understand this as you begin working out the dart control in the patterns.

No matter how many pieces you choose to cut this pattern into to create a design, if the proper seam allowances are carefully added and the garment is sewn properly, the finished garment will be the size of the original pattern. It is the same principle as the puzzle!!

The pattern you see on the next page is the type of miniature basic pattern that is used in the classes that I teach on Pattern Designing. This is used to work out all of the design cuts. You may trace this and use as a practice pattern.

THE BASIC PATTERN

Below you see the pieces that compose a Basic Pattern. It is also known as a Flat Pattern, which can be used to create any type of clothing other than pants. Body Pattern is another name that it is known by, because it fits the body snugly. In other words, it's you! So discard all those ill-fitting patterns you have and get to work making a pattern that really fits. Then everything you make, you'll love.

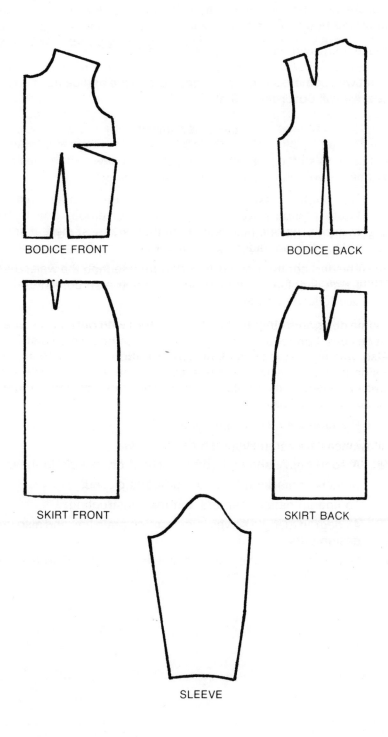

BODICE FRONT   BODICE BACK

SKIRT FRONT   SKIRT BACK

SLEEVE

PATTERN TALK

NOW THE FUN BEGINS

"What We Hope Ever To Do With Ease, We Must Learn
First To Do With Diligence." ...Johnson

How true this statement by Mr. Johnson is. Remember how hard your first algebra problem was, or the first date you went on, or the first dress you made, or any of the other firsts in your life? We would never progress if we gave up from our many first tries. So keep this in mind and, before you know it, you will be designing patterns with ease. And the fun doesn't end.

Let's start out with some really easy designs. Since the bodice front undergoes the most design changes, we will cover these first.

LET'S GET SHIFTY

We will first learn to shift dart positions to achieve a new pattern design, but before we tackle our first design, we must understand a few rudiments.

Dart Control: Dart control, as we have said before, is the manner in which we cope with figure contour. We must, however, remember one thing. To shift *dart control* from one position to another, we must start at some seam: waist, side, neck, shoulder, etc., and work to the *Dart Control Point*.

Dart Control Point: The dart control point is found by intersecting the waist dart and side dart, which is actually the bust point. This is also considered your high point. See following page.

Dart Legs: Dart legs are the angle lines that form the dart.

TOOLS OF THE TRADE

The tools you will need to make your pattern designs can be kept simple. These are the basics that are sufficient for your needs.

Ruler   Preferably a clear plastic one.

Pencils   Two colors, to distinguish design cuts.

Tape Measure   A good heavy one that you can stand on its side to measure curves.

Tape   Scotch or masking tape to tape darts closed.

Yardstick   To line up pattern centers and for constructing.

Triangle   45-degree triangle serves to determine grain line and also helps in lining up design cuts.

French Curve   Optional. I find they are limited in working pattern curves. Sketching curves really works best.

DART CONTROL

Dart Control is determined by measuring the high and low points and subtracting the difference. For instance: If the bust (high point) is 34 inches and the waist (low point) is 24 inches (to make it easy), the dart control will be 10 inches, or the difference. This 10 inches has to be used by distributing to one or more areas.

Better fit is accomplished by measuring the front and back of the body separately. You will do this when you make your basic pattern. Let's say that you have measured your bodice front and the bustline measures 19 inches and the waistline measures 13 inches. This means that you have 6 inches of dart control to be utilized on the bodice front.

Below you see a bodice front with the various high and low points. The larger dot represents the *high point*. The lines lead to areas that yield to dart control. These are *low points*.

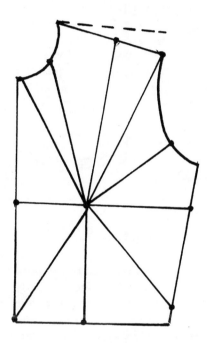

As you can see, dart control is also used at the shoulder and side to fit the high and low points of the body. The shoulder dart control is not taken from your 6 inches but the side dart control is. You will learn how to determine the shoulder dart control when you make your basic pattern.

The various dart control positions allow versatility in designing. You will learn how to use all of these dart control positions in the following pattern designs.

Aren't you excited?!

PATTERN TALK

PATTERN CONSTRUCTION

To design from a basic pattern and make changes to achieve various designs, you are constructing a pattern. So, a basic pattern that has been changed is called a Construction Pattern.

After you have completed your Construction Pattern, you will make a Final Pattern and add all seam allowances. I make Final Patterns directly on the fabric itself, eliminating a lot of work. It also makes cutting the garment much easier.

EXAMPLE:

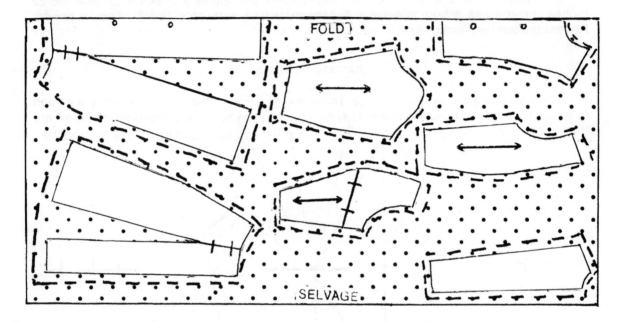

Lay your Construction Pattern on your fabric. Weight down pattern. Draw cutting lines (seam allowances) with tailor's chalk or thin pieces of soap (thin soap makes excellent chalk and wipes off easily — besides, you won't have to feel guilty about throwing the soap away). Draw in your darts, pleat or gathering information. Draw 5/8 inch seams with the exception of areas which would later be trimmed: neck, armhole, etc. Use 3/8 inch seams for these areas and you will eliminate trimming later. Most tape measures actually measure 5/8 inches wide, so it's quite easy to lay your tape measure against the edge of your pattern and draw or dot along your seams.

Now for the good part! After drawing your Construction Pattern onto the fabric, remove pattern and cut on drawn lines. You will find this method is far easier than trying to cut your fabric with the pattern pinned or weighted to it.

HOW MUCH YARDAGE?

With the high cost of good fabric, it is very important to buy only what is needed to construct a garment. The easiest way to establish the needed quantity is to use newspapers (here we go again) to simulate the fabric. Newspapers measure 23 inches by 30 inches (generally). Therefore, if you are planning to use 60-inch fabric for your garment, lay newspaper on the floor with the 30 inches crosswise. You may need several pieces stretched out. Label one side Fold and the other Selvage. Now place your Constructed Pattern on the paper so that all the paper is used effectively. Measure the amount of newspaper you've used. This represents yardage required.

If 45-inch fabric is to be used, turn newspapers the opposite direction so that the 23 inches is crosswise. Make allowance for the extra half-inch (only 22-1/2 inches is used). Repeat the above procedure.

PATTERN SYMBOLS

To understand the various changes made on the basic patterns in our lessons, we need to establish certain symbols to use so that the changes can be readily understood. Below are the various changes and their symbols that you will be observing in the following lessons.

DART CONTROL POINT	CONSTRUCTION CHANGES	CLOSED DART
+	- - - -	┼┼

FILLED-IN AREAS	DISCARDED AREAS	PATTERN CHANGE POSITIONS
		● ● ● ●

ADDED SEAM ALLOWANCE	CUT ON BIAS	PLACE ON FOLD
• • • •		o o

HOW TO FIND THE GRAIN LINE

Although the grain line, or straight of goods, is important in clothes construction, don't feel that everything you make has to be cut with the straight of grain. Very effective designing can be achieved with crosswise and bias cutting.

When separating a pattern for a special design, you must carry out the grain line in each pattern piece. Below are illustrations to show how it's done.

To determine grain line:

1. Measure from center front at two points on pattern, making each same distance from center.

2. Draw a line to intersect these two points. This is the lengthwise grain.

3. Draw lines from center front to points. These are crosswise grain lines.

4. To obtain the true bias, bisect the crosswise and lengthwise grain lines. This will be a 45-degree angle.

To determine grain line for pattern pieces to be separated:

1. Using Step #1 above, find two points in the section that will be separated.

2. Repeat #2 above for lengthwise grain.

3. Repeat #3 above for crosswise grain.

4. Repeat #4 above for the bias grain.

5. Pattern is now ready to be separated.

For Sleeve: Draw straight line from cap line. Proceed with above steps.

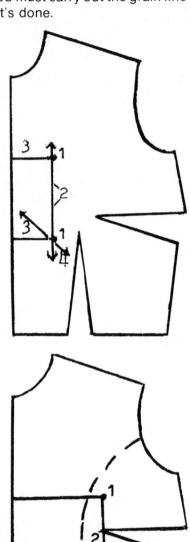

Yes, darts really give our garments personality. Variety is needed to feel that we're not wearing the same thing over and over again. This chapter teaches you how to use darts effectively to enhance your designs. Let's do something really easy for a start. We will use a back basic pattern this time and we are going to change the dart control to the neckline. Why make a neck dart? Well, sometimes it's more flattering and, if the dress has a Queen Anne neckline (as you see below), it shapes the neckline better. Also, if you are making a scoop neck, it gives a closer fit. Shoulder darts on a scoop neckline look awkward.

NECK DART

Pattern Construction:

1. Dot dart position on neckline.

2. Draw a 4-inch line that points toward the **waist** dart.

3. Draw a line from the end of this line to the shoulder dart.

4. Cut lines.

5. Pull shoulder dart together and tape.

You now have a new neckline dart.

To Sew: If you are using this dart on a Queen Anne neckline, you will want to do one **important thing.** **The portion of the** dart that stands up on the neck (portion that has been added on) should be sewn straight, then the dart from there down will be sewn at an angle. If you don't do this, the neckline will not lay smoothly.

FOLDED DART

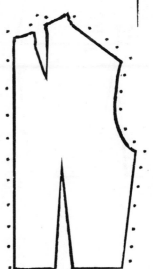

DART PERSONALITY

FRONT SHOULDER DART

This dart is often used on jackets, coats and housecoats. It will be the only dart control the garment has. The garment hangs loosely from the bust down and gives a free-flowing effect.

Pattern Construction:

1. Find dart point.

2. Dot dart position. Generally the dart is positioned at center shoulder but many times will be used about 1 inch from the neck.

3. Draw new dart line from dart position to the dart control point.

4. Draw line to side dart.

5. Cut on lines.

6. Tape side dart.

7. Draw a new dart point about 2 inches above the control point. This gives a softer effect.

8. Fill in waist dart.

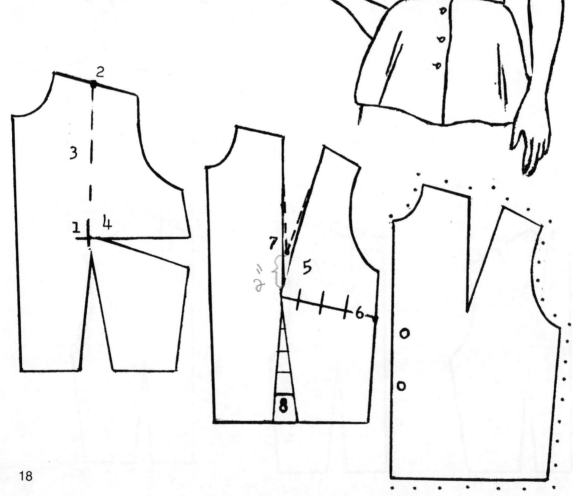

ARMHOLE DART

This dart is very attractive on a one-piece dress when only bust control is desired — in a chemise or sheath design, for instance.

Pattern Construction:

1. Find dart control point.

2. Dot position of new dart, usually at the area just above where the arm joins the body.

3. Draw new dart, from armhole to control point.

4. Draw line to side dart.

5. Cut lines.

6. Tape side dart closed.

7. Draw new dart point about 1/2 to 1 inch above dart control point. It will depend upon size of bust.

8. Fill in waist dart.

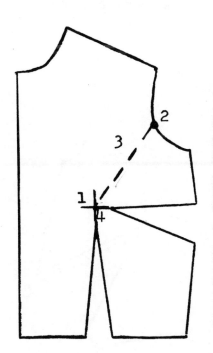
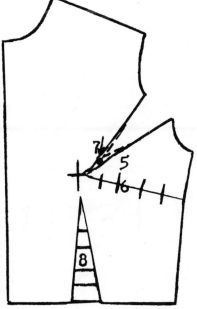
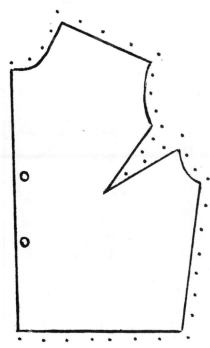

DART PERSONALITY

FRENCH DART

This is a very flattering dart to be used either as a single or double dart. If you have a particularly pretty floral or plaid, the French dart will allow the fabric to remain uninterrupted in the front of the garment.

SINGLE FRENCH DART

Pattern Construction:

1. Mark dart control point on basic bodice front.

2. Draw from control point to waist and side darts.

3. Draw a line at an angle from the control point to about 2 to 3 inches above waist at side of pattern. Depends upon effect you desire.

4. Cut on lines.

5. Pull waist and side darts together and tape.

6. Curve waistline to smooth pattern.

See the results!! You have created a brand new dart that is a combination of the two.

Since this dart is such a large dart, it is better to use seam allowance around the dart. This eliminates bulk and is easier to sew.

To Sew: Darts lay better if you start at the point and sew outward. Take three stitches at the point very close to the folded edge of the dart to eliminate puckering which is so unsightly. The Single French Dart should be sewn all the way to the bust point.

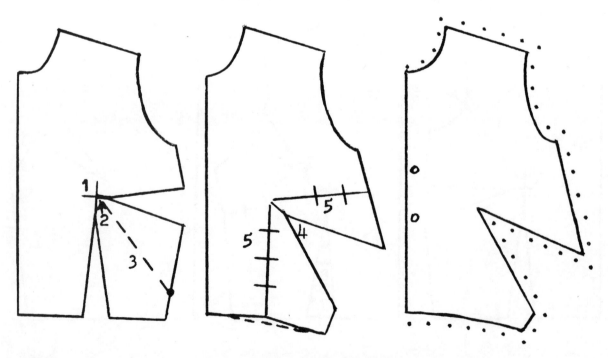

DOUBLE FRENCH DART

Several years ago, I bought a luscious shrimp-colored wool fabric. I designed a dress with a double French dart, used a Queen Anne neckline, a squared raglan sleeve and added a leopard belt (which I made). I also pulled some of the threads of the fabric and did a hand stitch around the armholes. Talk about compliments!!

Pattern Construction:

1. Find dart control point.

2. Draw two new darts 2 inches apart, forming an arrow at the bust point.

3. Cut arrow out. Pull waist dart and side bust dart together and tape. You have left a large opening.

4. Lay your arrow into this space to form two new darts on either side of the arrow.

5. Draw your new darts beginning 1 inch from dart control point.

Now, that wasn't so hard, was it?

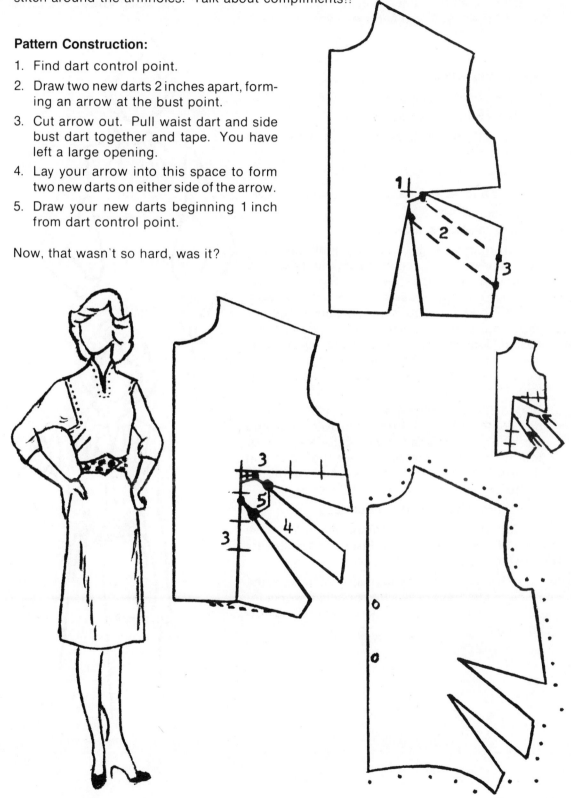

MULTIPLE NECK DARTS

With the next two lessons, you will learn to handle multiple darts. This is called the sunburst design — very pretty on a blouse, a formal dress or wedding gown. You may also use folded darts here rather than stitched ones. They should be folded toward the center neck. For effect, you also can make your darts on the outside of the dress.

Pattern Construction:

1. Find dart control point.

2. Dot position of new dart control.

3. Draw line from neck to control point and to waist and side darts.

4. Cut lines.

5. Pull side and waist darts together. Your dart control is now at the neck.

6. Fill this empty space with paper.

7. In making this design, I have found that it works best to have only 1 inch in the sunburst darts for the bottom of the darts to work out smoothly. So, if you are making the seven-dart design, you want 7 inches of dart control at the neckline. My basic works out perfectly for this. If I do the five-dart design, I close only the side dart and this gives me the 5 inches I need. You can use more dart control for the folded darts, so I usually use the maximum for these.

8. Draw center dart 5 inches long and use 1/2 of your dart control which is 1/2 inch. Go over 1 inch and mark another inch dart — repeat for the third or fourth dart. Find the centers for the darts and draw second one 4-1/2 inches long, the third 4 inches long, and the fourth 3-1/2 inches long.

9. Draw the dart legs and cut out darts.

Aren't you proud of your accomplishment? I have made all three types of this design and was very happy with the effect of all of them.

NOTE: The second model has sunburst tucks at the neckline of the dress. The same principle works for this dress, but see pages on tucks to understand how to treat them.

MULTIPLE NECK DARTS

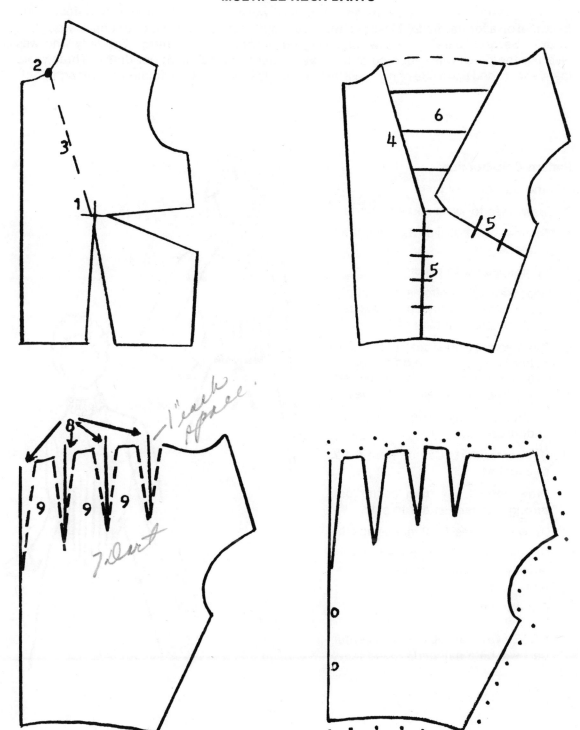

DART PERSONALITY

EMPIRE WAIST DARTS

This design is an empire, using a series of waist darts to complete the effect. Very beautiful on a formal dress. Makes up well in any soft (but not flimsy) fabric such as wool, knit or silk. Several years ago, I saw this design used on a sheath dress. The lady who was wearing the dress was shopping and I stopped her to compliment her dress. Three years later, she turned up in one of my dress designing classes. It was an immediate recognition!

Pattern Construction:

1. Find dart control point.

2. Draw lines to waist and side darts.

3. Cut lines and pull side dart together and tape.

4. Fill in space with paper.

5. Measure dart control and multiply by 2. For demonstration, we will use 3-1/2 inches for a total of 7.

6. This design works best if only 3/4 inches is used in each dart. Therefore, we will have 1-3/4 inches left over. This will be taken off sides.

7. Measure body from waist to underbust. Dot.

8. Dot center dart. Can be from 5-1/2 to 6 inches.

9. Draw angled line from center dot through underbust dot to side.

10. Draw four lines 1-1/2 inches apart.

11. Draw darts, dividing the 3/4 inches equally on either side of dart centers.

12. Cut out darts.

    NOTE: On #10 above, the center dart will be a half dart.

EMPIRE WAIST DARTS

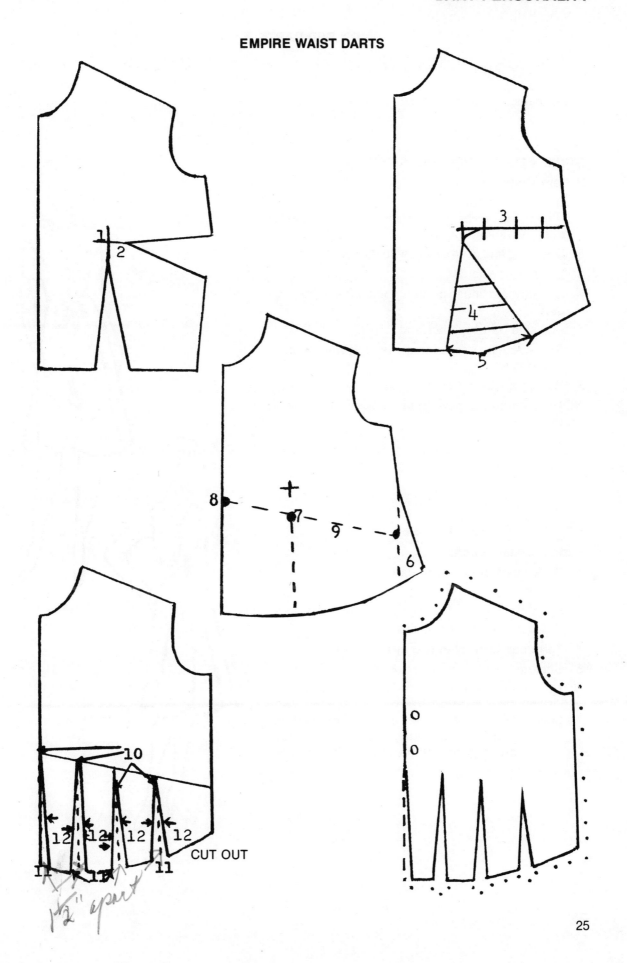

CUT OUT

1½" apart

DART PERSONALITY

FOLDED DARTS

Folded darts have a personality all their own. They are folded instead of sewn, which gives a soft look to a dress. They are especially effective when soft fabrics such as lightweight wools, silks, voiles, or soft polyesters are used.

STYLE #1 — FOLDED SHOULDER
Pattern Construction:

1. Determine style line for neck. A round scooped or V-neckline can be used. We'll do a V-neckline for demonstration. Cut off.
2. Draw fold line from shoulder to dart control point.
3. Fill in waistline dart.
4. Cut dart fold line to control point and then to side dart.
5. Pull side dart together and tape.
6. Give waistline control to center and side. Cut off sections.
7. Repeat for back. See diagram.

NOTE: You do not have to use a center front seam on this style.

STYLE #2 — WAIST FOLDS
Pattern Construction:

1. Draw line from waist to dart control point.
2. Cut line to control point and to both side and waistline darts.
3. Pull darts together and tape.
4. Form dart control in two or more folds.
5. Change neckline to V-neckline.

NOTE: You must use a center seam for this style.

To Sew: For both styles: fold dart control as arrows indicate. Stay-stitch to secure before proceeding with the rest of the garment.

STYLE #1

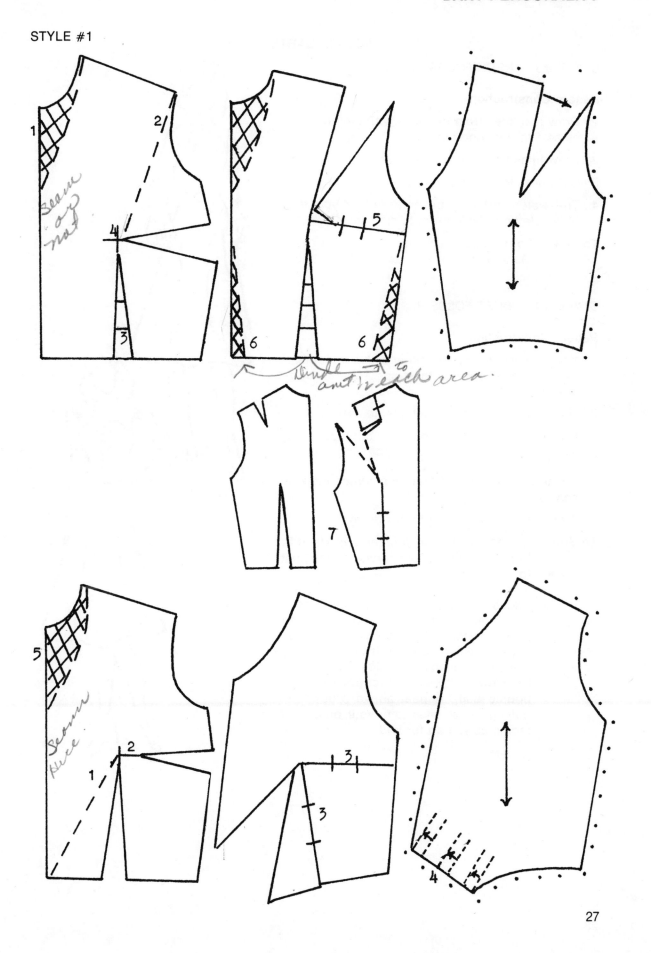

DART PERSONALITY

FOLDED DARTS

STYLE #3 — NECK FOLDS

Pattern Construction:

1. Draw two lines from the neck with the line closest to the center longer.

2. Draw lines from these to side dart.

3. Cut lines. Pull side dart together and tape.

4. The waist dart may be gathered or you may eliminate and give control to side seam.

To Sew: Form folds away from center neck. Machine baste. Sew as usual.

STYLE #4 — BUST FOLDS

Pattern Construction:

1. You may use this design either with a sweetheart neckline or a dress with straps. Decide upon design.

2. Draw line from center bust to side dart.

3. Cut line. Pull side dart together and tape.

4. Close waistline dart.

5. Divide waistline control between center and side seams.

6. A center seam is a must in this design.

To Sew: Lay bodice half on yourself and stand in front of a mirror. Fold darts between bust to fit bustline perfectly. Repeat for other side, matching the dart folds. Sew center seams together. Cut facing at this time in the sweetheart shape that has been formed by the folds. Facing will shape the neckline when you sew it on. You may use *gathers* instead of folds if you wish. Sew three rows of stitching on each bodice half. Repeat above procedure, pulling the stitches to fit your bust. Cut facing as you do for folds.

STYLE #3

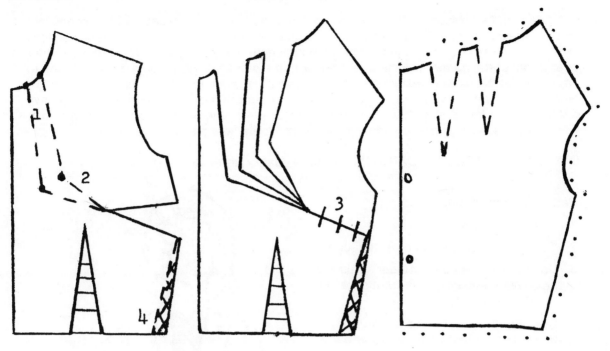

STYLE #4

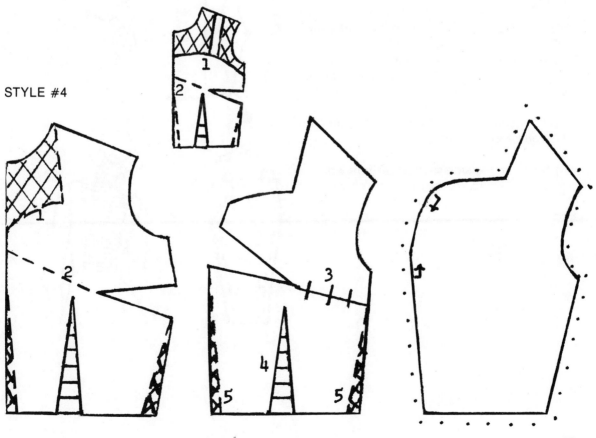

DISCERNING DIVIDED DARTS

PRINCESS SEAMS

The next few lessons will teach how to divide dart control into seams. The seams are actually used to control figure contour in the place of darts. Since they are shaped seams, excellent fit and unusual designs can be accomplished. The seams extend from the shoulder or armhole of the garment to the waistline, or to the hemline. They give a designed look to any garment. Many well-designed suits use this type of seam to achieve exceptional fit. To be effective, a fabric with body is needed to construct the design. However, you will have difficulty if the fabric has little or no give, such as corduroy, hard cottons or other tightly woven fabrics, since there is some easing in fitting the sections together.

STYLE #1 — SHOULDER DART (This design is flattering to almost every figure.)

Pattern Construction:

1. Find dart control point.

2. Find straight of grain for outside section.

3. Dot control point on shoulder. This can be anywhere from 1 inch from shoulder to center shoulder.

4. Draw line from shoulder to dart control point. Draw lines to waist and side darts.

5. Cut lines. Pull side dart together and tape.

6. You now have two pattern sections with which to work.

7. Repeat for back.

NOTE: You have a gap at the front of your side dart. This will work out in easing in most cases. If you find that you have too much to cope with, cut excess off at shoulder. See diagram #8. This will not affect the fit. If you have too much fullness under the bust, you may take this off as diagram #9 indicates.

To Sew: Ease side sections as you would a sleeve before attaching to center section.

STYLE #1

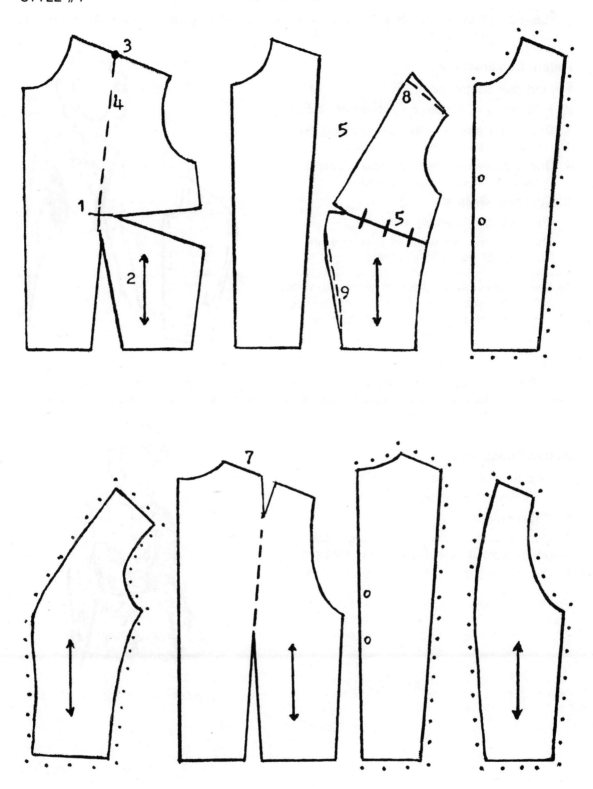

DISCERNING DIVIDED DARTS

PRINCESS SEAMS

STYLE #2 — This over-the-bust Princess seam is very flattering and works well in both suits and dresses.

Pattern Construction:

1. Find dart control point.
2. Find straight of grain on outside of bodice.
3. Dot your armhole — this depends on height, generally about 4 inches from shoulder.
4. Draw a curved line from armhole to control point. Draw lines to waist and side darts.
5. Cut lines. Separate.
6. Pull side dart together and tape.
7. The back will not have as curved a line as the front. It will be more shallowed.

To Sew: Sew easing stitch to seam allowance on the side curve. Ease to fit center section. Press and sew sections together.

STYLE #3 — This design is very attractive if you plan to use trim or if you use two colors or two different fabrics. For instance: A solid on the sides and a striped, plaid, floral or eyelet in the center.

Pattern Construction:

1. Find dart control point.
2. Find straight of grain.
3. Dot shoulder.
4. Draw line from shoulder through dart control point to waist dart. Draw line to side dart.
5. Cut on lines, pull side dart together and tape.

STYLE #2

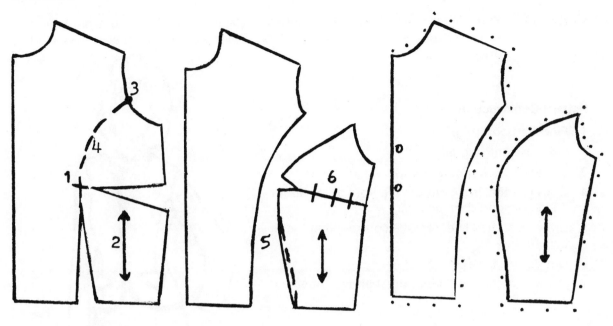

BODICE BACK

STYLE #3

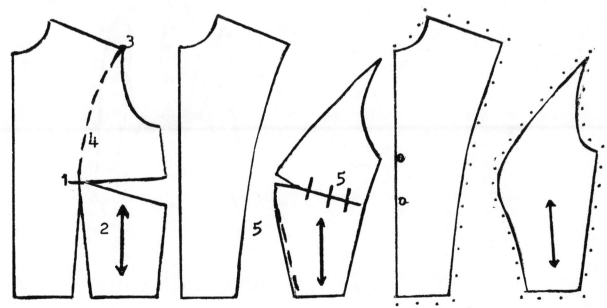

DISCERNING DIVIDED DARTS

PRINCESS SEAMS

STYLE #4 — This Princess seam is one of my favorites. Designers will use it for a number of years and then it will disappear for a time. This design works best in an easy-fit dress or jacket.

Pattern Construction:

1. Find dart control point.
2. Find straight of grain.
3. Dot armhole at point of curve.
4. Draw line that is slightly curved from dot to about 1 inch beyond the waist dart.
5. Draw an angled line from the control point to the curved line.
6. Cut on lines. Separate.
7. Pull waist and side darts together and tape.

You can see that you have formed a new dart. This dart should always be sewn all the way to the bust point. It will ruin the effect of the design if it rides above or below the bust point.

To Sew: Sew new dart first. Then follow directions for Style #2.

STYLE #5 — Very attractive. Why not try this one?

Pattern Construction:

1. Find dart control point.
2. Find straight of grain.
3. Dot position of design at neck.
4. Draw line from neck dot to control point.
5. Cut on line. Separate.
6. Pull side dart together and tape.

To Sew: You may need to interface the center section if your fabric has stretch. This will secure the fabric and the design will be smoother. Sew easing stitch on outside section before attaching to center section.

STYLE #4

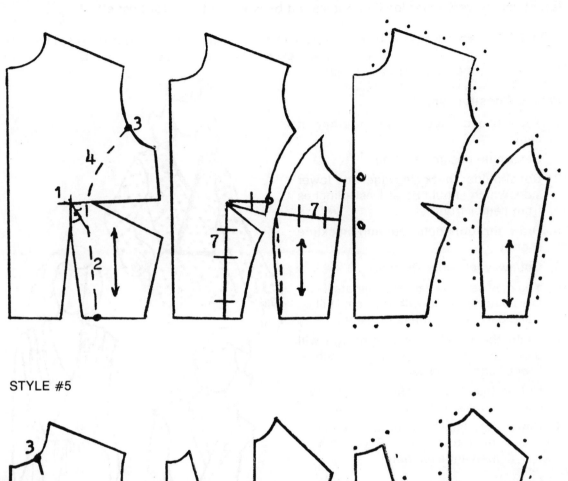

STYLE #5

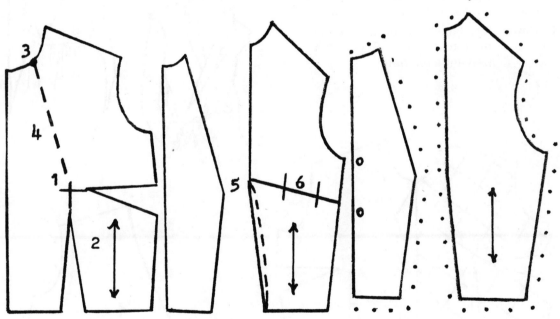

DOUBLE-BREASTED BEAUTIES

Double-breasted dresses, jackets and coats can give a change of pace in styling. There are many variations, but they are basically all styled as the ones below. A double-breasted jacket can be very smart looking but should be worn buttoned for best effect.

STYLE #1 — This design, known as the wrap front, is flattering to all figures except the very heavy. Variations can be achieved to get the effect you desire. Directions are the same for each variation.

Pattern Construction:

1. Tape two bodice fronts together at center.

2. Determine design variation.

3. Dot shoulder, neck cleavage, and lower side, which should be at least 4 inches from center front.

4. Draw through dots, curving neckline slightly.

5. Cut away left side. Discard.

6. You may use side dart or eliminate if you are using a fabric with stretch. Fill in waist dart. Use gathers or pleats.

7. Often the neckline of this design will gap. To avoid, cut off 1/2 to 1 inch at lower edge of bodice.

8. Cut on bias for best effect. Not necessary if fullness is used at shoulder.

To Sew: Interface neckline with it placed next to bodice. Stay-stitch to prevent stretching.

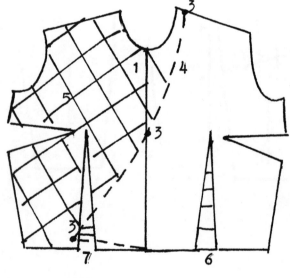

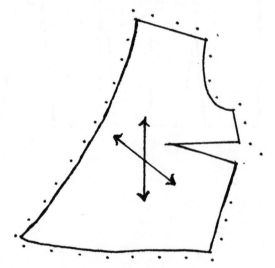

STYLE #2 — This double-breasted design has many variations and can be used on dresses, jackets and coats. It is not flattering to the large figure.

Pattern Construction:

1. Tape two bodice fronts together at center.

2. Dot design. Sketch in.

3. Draw size of button you will be using. This is very important. You want to get the total effect. Buttons also determine where your buttonholes will be. See "buttons" in "Finishing Touch" chapter.

4. Cut away right side. Discard.

NOTE:

It is not necessary to cut two sections (A) for bodice if you only plan to use buttonholes at opening. Use (B) for left side. Eliminates bulkiness. Buttons on right side of bodice will be sewn on for effect.

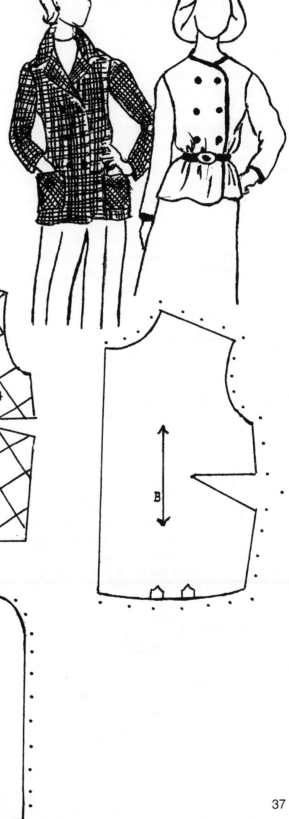

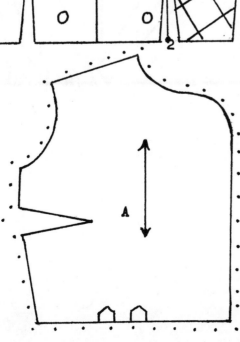

GATHERS . . . PLEATS . . . TUCKS

Gathers are flattering to almost every figure and can cover many figure faults. The softness of gathers gives a very feminine look. Pleats and tucks can be used for design effect. Styles using gathers are almost limitless. Gathers around bust area can give a small bust more proportion and provides softness for the full bust.

STYLE #1 — THE BLOUSON (It is soft and flattering to most all figures.)

Pattern Construction:

1. Draw line between side and waist darts.
2. Pull side dart together and tape.
3. Add 1/2 to 1 inch to the bottom for blouson effect. If you wish more gathers, you must add additional amount to the side — note diagram.

STYLE #2 — This design shows how to use a yoke with gathers over the bust. It is very effective if two colors are used; or you may wish to use bias checks on the yoke for design effect.

Pattern Construction:

1. Draw yoke, allowing 2-1/2 inches for the width of the half flap and 1-1/2 to 2 inches for the depth.
2. Draw lines to waist and side darts.
3. Cut lines and tape darts.
4. Fill in cut-out flap section. Fill in cut-out section for gathers.
5. Make facing pattern for flap.

To Sew: Flap should be finished before attaching yoke to bottom. Sew facing to flap, trim and clip corners and turn. Sew from clipped corners outward when attaching to bottom section.

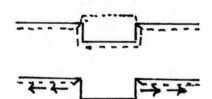

STYLE #1

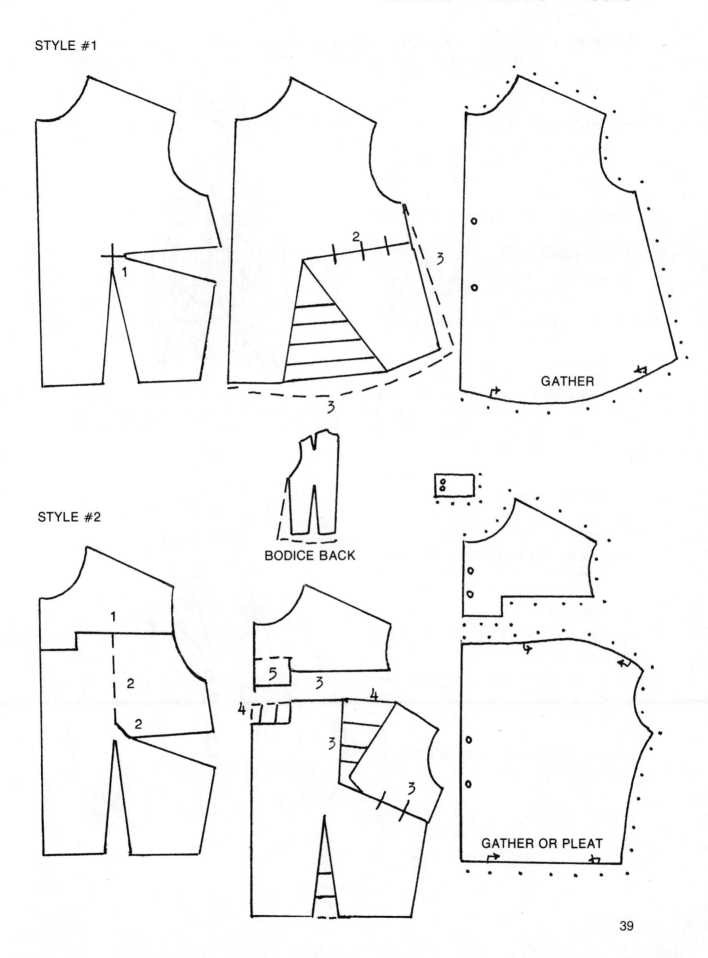

STYLE #2

BODICE BACK

GATHER

GATHER OR PLEAT

GATHERS . . . PLEATS . . . TUCKS

STYLE #3 — The design in this style allows you to have gathers over the bust, which is flattering but does not interfere with the center focus of the dress. This design also shows how to handle a *dart slice*.

Pattern Construction:

1. Draw lines. Begin your horizontal line 2-1/2 inches from center over to armhole. Draw lines to waist and side darts.

2. Cut lines, pull together side dart, and tape.

3. Fill in space.

To Sew: This is to be treated as a dart. Gather area on bottom, pull to fit top. Fold together and pin. Starting at dart point, sew outward.

STYLE #4 — Here we see a similarity with Style #3. We use a dart slice to achieve fullness under the bust but leave the center front undisturbed. This looks well on blouses or dresses with front opening. It gives a tailored look with a feminine approach.

Pattern Construction:

1. Measure yourself from waist to under-bust.

2. Dot under-bust area. Dot 2 inches from center front and 5 inches from waist. Dot 3 to 4 inches at side from waist.

3. Draw between dots.

4. Draw line between waist and side darts.

5. Cut lines.

6. Pull waist and side darts together and tape.

7. If you wish additional fullness, add at side.

To Sew: Follow directions for Style #3.

STYLE #3

STYLE #4

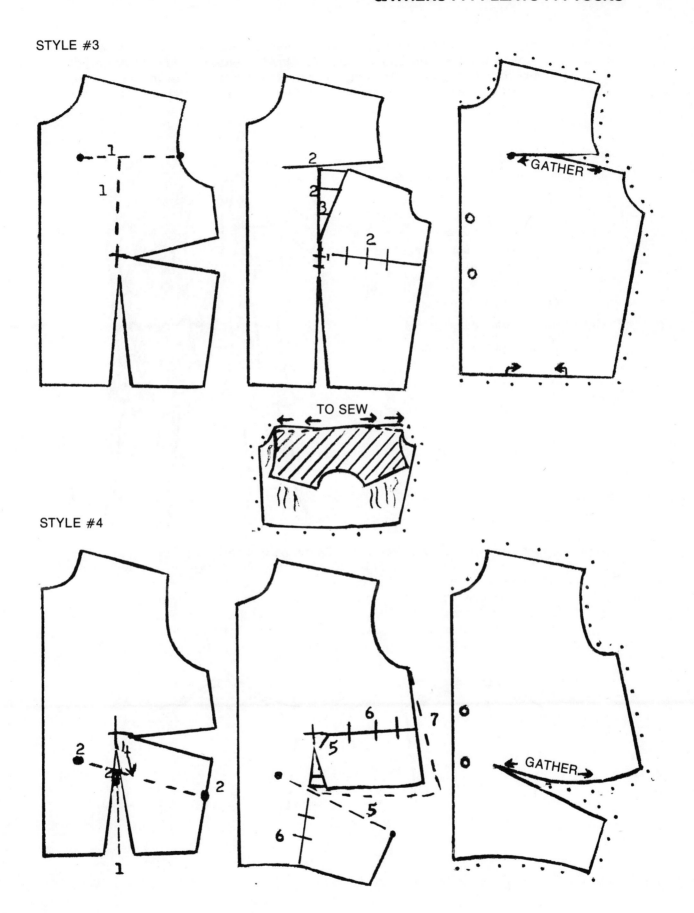

GATHERS . . . PLEATS . . . TUCKS

STYLE #5 — You will learn to make an Empire Waist with this design. Also, you will be adding gathers to the under-bust area. Fitted empires should be worn only by the trim, but looser-fitting empires can be worn by all but the very large. Directions for easy-fitting empires is found in the chapter on "One-Piece Dresses."

Pattern Construction:

1. Measure yourself from waist to area under the bust.

2. Draw between waist and side dart. Cut.

3. Pull waist together and tape.

4. Dot closed dart with measurement from Item #1.

5. Draw a curved or pointed yoke, drawing through above measurement.

6. Cut on line. Separate.

7. Pull side dart together and tape.

8. Dart space may be used for gathers, pleats or tucks. Add to side for more gathers.

To Sew: Empire yokes fit better if interfaced. Gather bodice to fit yoke. Sew from center front outward. In sewing a pointed yoke to obtain a definite point, sew beginning 1/2 inch from center, outward. Turn dress and finish the point by hand-sewing. Points will have to be clipped and trimmed for smooth fit. Oh, there's something else — midriffs need to fit snugly, so after you cut the midriff out, pin front and back together at sides and make adjustment. Gather bodice to fit.

STYLE #5

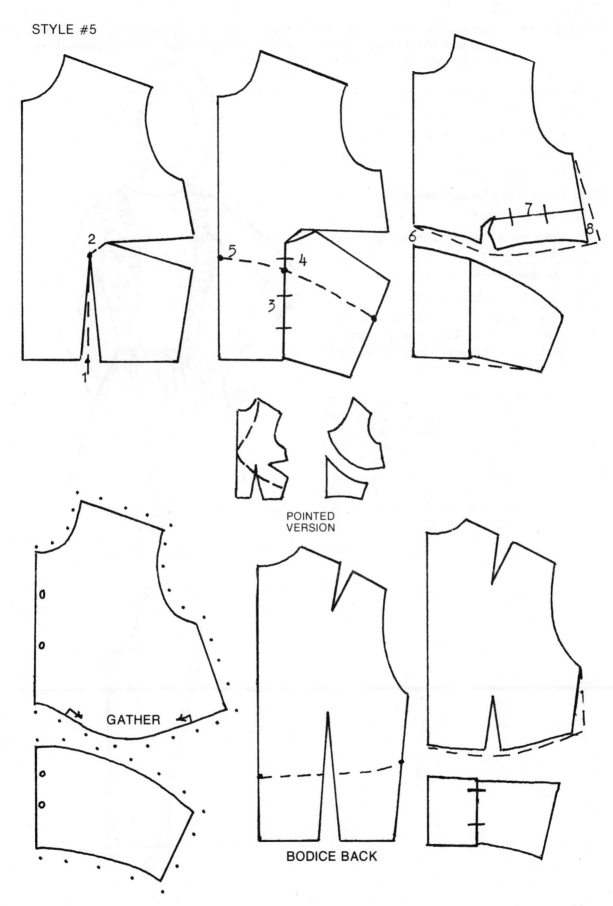

POINTED
VERSION

GATHER

BODICE BACK

STYLE #6 — This style is a real eye-catcher. Admiring glances will be yours. This is to be used with sheer fabrics as the sides will be shirred. Sew a softly gathered skirt onto the bodice and you have a winner!!

Pattern Construction:

1. Find dart control point.

2. Dot 1-1/2 inches from shoulder. Draw through dart control to waist dart.

3. Cut line. Separate.

4. Cut a lining for both sections.

5. Fill in side dart.

6. Draw eight lines horizontally across the side section.

7. Number the sections; cut on lines.

8. Pull apart. Spread evenly.

9. If you are using very sheer fabric, you will want to allow three times width of sections. Otherwise, twice the width of the sections is sufficient.

To Sew: Sew dart in side section of lining. Sew gathering stitches on the front, side and armhole of side section of bodice. Pull gathers so that it will fit the lining. Stay-stitch together. Place center section to lining and stay-stitch. Sew front and side sections together.

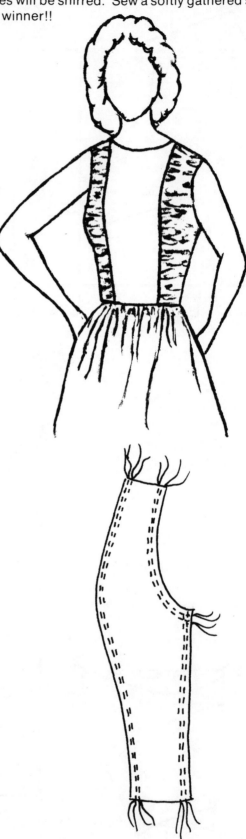

STYLE #6

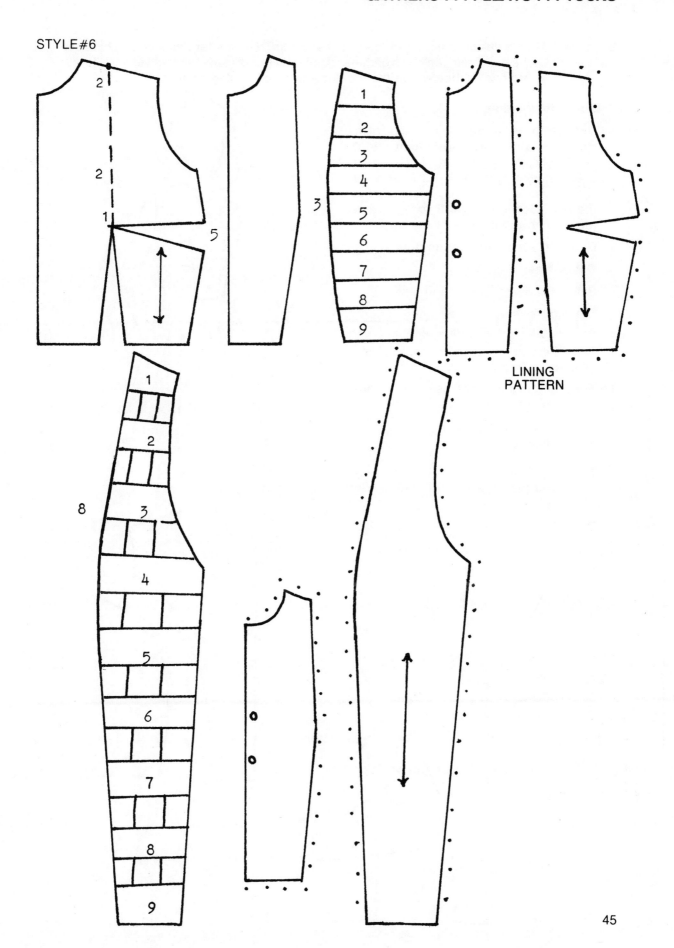

LINING
PATTERN

GATHERS . . . PLEATS . . . TUCKS

STYLE #7 — This design is a form of the Princess Seam. The center panel sets in between the bust area and gives gathers to the bust for ease and attractiveness. This is especially effective on the medium- to small-busted figure.

Pattern Construction:

1. Dot armhole about 4 inches from shoulder. Dot inside bust point about 1-1/2 inches from center front. This is for average bust span of 7-1/2 inches. If your span is wider, you may want 2 inches. Dot waist 1-1/2 to 2 inches (depending upon the bust span dot).

2. Draw a curved line through dots.

3. Cut on line. Separate.

4. Pull waist dart together and tape.

5. Draw three lines across side section. Cut to within 1/4 inches of side.

6. Pull side dart together and tape. Open lines to desired fullness.

To Sew: Interface front section if your fabric is not firm. Gather side section to fit front. Sew from front section to assure smooth finish.

NOTE: Clip front section; notch side section as diagram shows. Your pieces will fit together smoothly as a result.

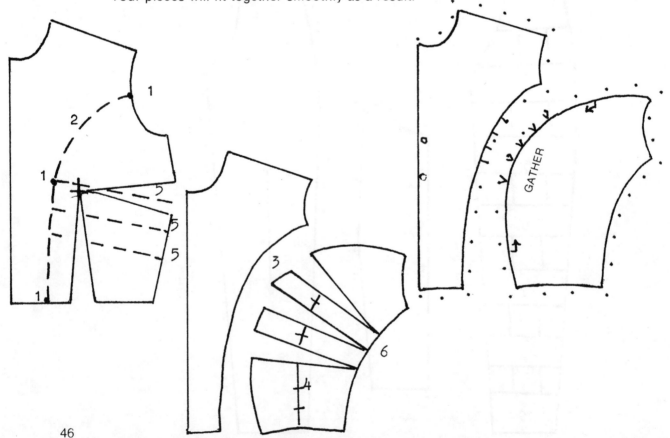

STYLE #8 — BACK YOKE WITH GATHERS: We are going to change pace and work on a bodice back. This design is just what you need to give a shirtwaist dress a little extra class. You are also getting a lesson on yokes as well as a lesson on gathers.

Pattern Construction:

1. Dot down about 4 inches from center neck.

2. Place ruler at dot, with side against center back. Draw a line to armhole.

3. Cut on line. Separate.

4. Draw line to waist dart. Cut.

5. Pull apart to desired fullness.

6. Correct shoulder dart control. Refer to the "Shirtwaist" section for directions.

To Sew: Sew two rows of gathering (7) stitches on both bottom and top of lower portion of bodice back. Pull to fit yoke and waist. Sew to yoke from center outward.

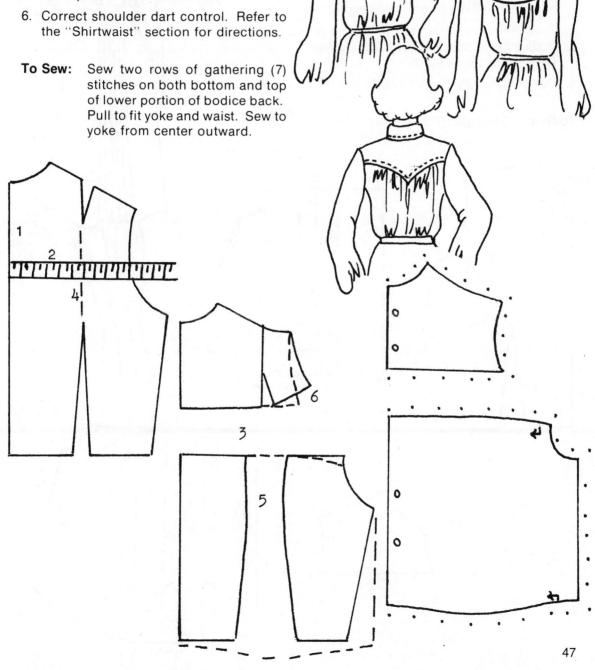

PLEATS

STYLE #1 — Pleats are a very effective way of adding design interest to clothing. Note this dress. It has pleat interest both on the bodice and on the skirt.

Pattern Construction:

1. Dot yoke — Draw.

2. Cut off. *yoke*

3. Draw line between waist and side darts.

4. Cut and treat as blouson.

5. Fill in space.

6. Determine how wide you want your pleats to be. If you want them to be 1/2 inch, then you will allow 1 inch per pleat.

7. Draw three lines from top to bottom of bodice 1 inch apart with the center line falling over the bust.

8. Cut on lines. Pull apart 1 inch. Fill in.

To Sew: Stitch pleats as you would for a tuck.

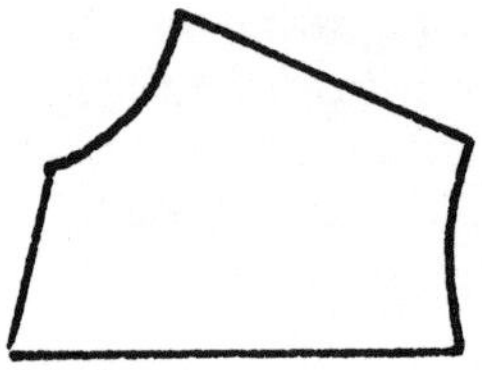

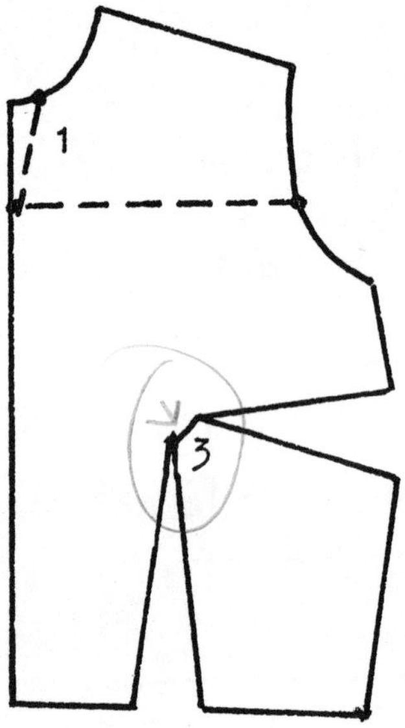

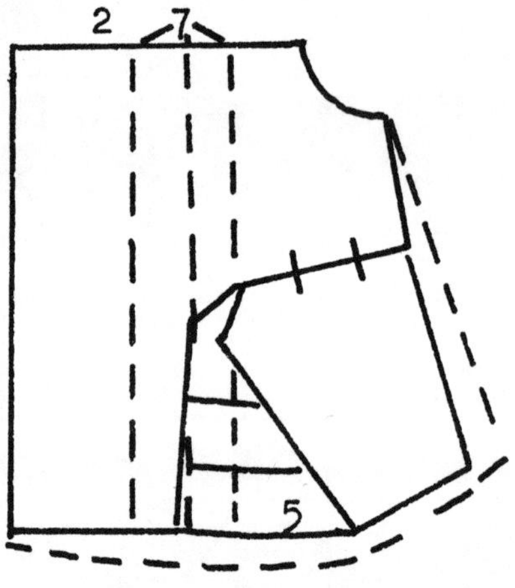

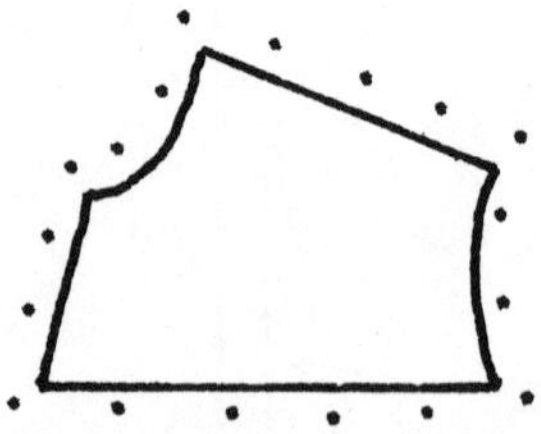

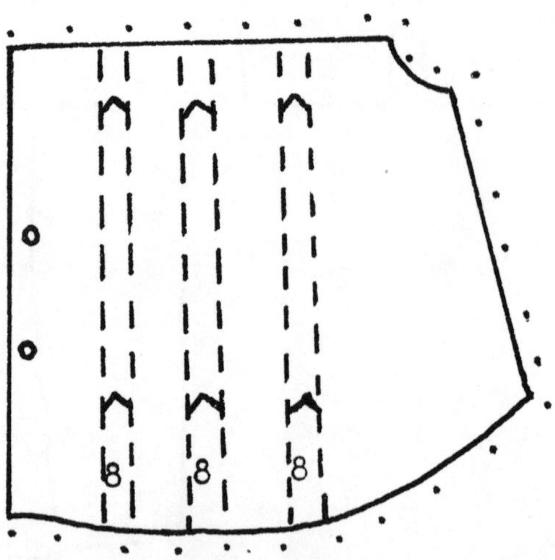

PLEATS

STYLE #2 — This style shows the back of a shirt-style dress in which pleats are used for interest. You may use with a straight or pointed yoke. We will use a pointed yoke to illustrate.

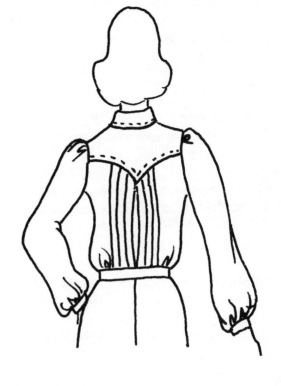

Pattern Construction:

1. Dot yoke with center dot being about 7 inches from neck. Dot armhole about 4 inches down.

2. Draw a curved line from dot to dot.

3. Cut on line. Separate.

4. Fill in waist dart.

5. Draw pleats on bottom of bodice. These pleat lines should be 1-1/4 inches apart.

6. Cut on lines. Separate.

7. Pull apart 2 inches.

8. Fill in. You will have to fill in 2 inches for center pleat also.

To Sew: Fold pleats toward center and pin at top and bottom. Sew along seam lines to secure. Sew to yoke, working from point outward.

REMEMBER: When working with pleats, you may use any amount in your folded pleats but you cannot exceed the amount of space between pleats. To do so will cause overlapping and bulkiness.

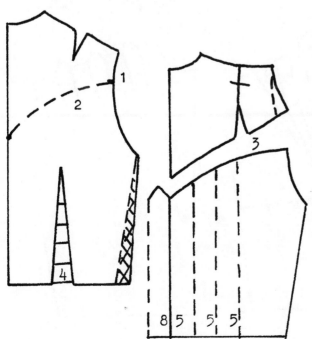

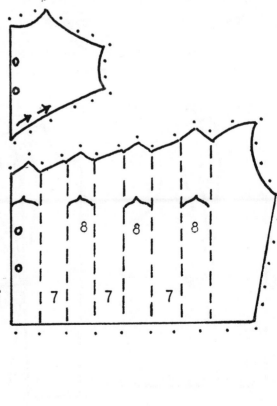

TUCKS

Open tucks are darts with the lower portion left unsewn to create a soft pleat at the end of the tuck. Effect is best when used on a soft fabric.

STYLE #1 — Instead of gathering the shoulder line, how about using a series of tucks. It will give a different look and will be a challenge to you.

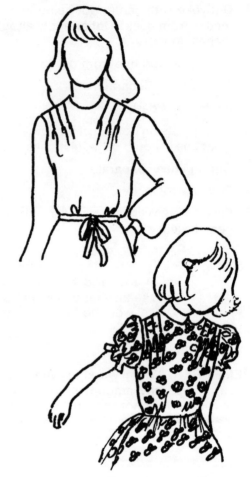

Pattern Construction:

1. Find dart control point.

2. Dot position of the number of tucks you wish to use, spacing them equally. We'll use three tucks for demonstration.

3. Draw center line from center dot to control point.

4. Draw lines approximately 3 to 4 inches long on either side of center line. Draw horizontal connecting line with the same slant as the shoulder.

5. Draw angle lines from the two side tucks to dart point. Draw line to side dart.

6. NUMBER SECTIONS. This is very important. Pieces can be transposed if not numbered.

7. Cut lines. Pull side dart together and tape.

8. Arrange tucks so they will have an equal amount in each.

To Sew: Fold tucks on markings and pin. Sew down to end of tucks. Secure stitches. Turn tucks toward shoulder and press.

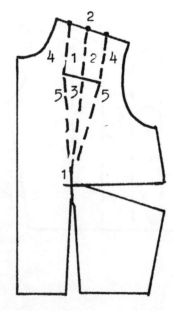

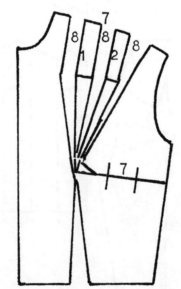

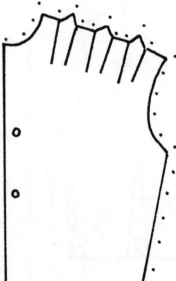

TUCKS

STYLE #2 — WAIST TUCKS: These can give a dress individuality. They also can dress up a plain dress or feminize a shirt dress.

Pattern Construction:

1. Find dart control points.

2. Draw line to side dart. Cut.

3. Pull waist dart together and tape.

4. Draw a line on dart line to control point.

5. Draw two lines parallel to the center line 3 to 4 inches long, depending on your height. Draw a horizontal line across the top of these. Draw angle lines to control point.

6. Cut lines and pull side dart together and tape.

7. Arrange tucks so they will have an equal amount in each.

To Sew: Follow directions for shoulder tucks.

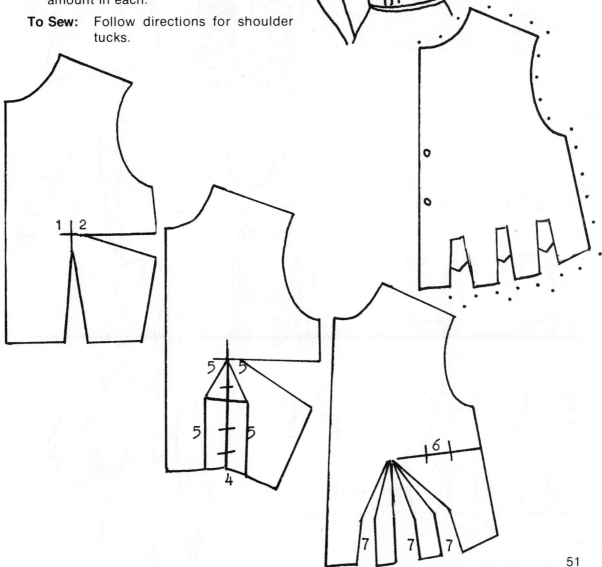

YOKES WITH A DIFFERENT STROKE

Yokes are versatile. They allow you to use your ingenuity and imagination. Also, it enables you to use fabric in which there is not enough yardage for a dress. When combined with a complimentary fabric, you can create a really beautiful dress. Several variations are worked out for you below, but don't limit yourself to these. This is one area in which you can be really creative.

STYLE #1 — These first yoke designs are simple and yet used so much by designers to give personality to a garment.

Pattern Construction:

1. Decide upon yoke design. Dot on bodice front and back if design is to be used on back.

2. Draw through dots.

3. Cut apart.

4. Cut facing for yoke.

To Sew: Follow instruction on Style #3.

NOTE: I made Design B for my triplets when they were five. I used olive green for the dresses with bone for the yoke, collar and cuffs. I piped the yoke and collar in burnt orange and covered buttons in burnt orange.

STYLE #2 — Rather than use a collar, why not use a yoke with a button and you will have a little individuality. It will also be cooler than a collar.

Pattern Construction:

1. Dot yoke 2 to 3 inches from neck. Repeat for back of bodice.

2. Draw through dots.

3. Mark center back and cut apart.

4. Tape front yoke to back yoke at shoulder.

5. Cut another yoke pattern from this. Tape together at center back so that you will have a complete pattern.

6. Add button extension to the right of the pattern.

7. Cut facing and interfacing for yoke.

To Sew: (a) Attach interfacing to upper part of inset. (b) Sew facing to this, sewing only the neckline and around the extension.
(c) Clip at end of extension.
(d) Turn yoke and press.
(e) Stay-stitch around bottom, keeping an equal distance from neckline. You can do this by measuring and dotting every few inches. This is so important for a smooth inset. (f) Pin to dress and sew on stay-stitching lines. Attach button.

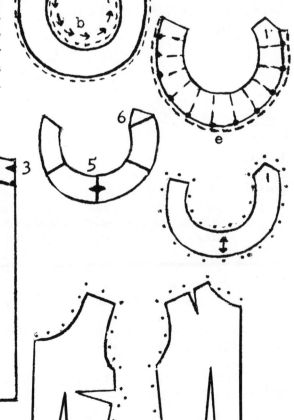

YOKES WITH A DIFFERENT STROKE

STYLE #3 — The yokes you see below are a little different from the ordinary, but they are yokes. I worked the first dress up in a plaid and used the background color for the yoke. I loved it!

Pattern Construction:

1. Dot yoke design. You'll have to decide upon width of yoke.

2. Draw through dots.

3. Cut apart.

4. Cut facing to fit yoke. Cut interfacing for yoke.

5. Repeat for back when design is used on the back.

For Lower Neckline for A: Determine shape of neckline and remove unneeded portion before working the design.

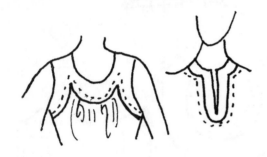

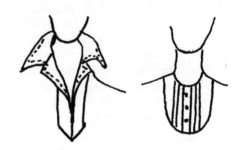

To Sew: In sewing yokes, you are working with a convex and a concave curve. The top or yoke is the convex curve and the bottom of the bodice is the concave. You are also working with a distinct point on some of the yokes. The secret of sewing the convex and the concave curves together is to allow only 3/8-inch seams. This eliminates bulkiness and will help you to get a better and more even curve. Always stay-stitch the convex side (with interfacing attached) on the 3/8-inch seam allowance, making sure your stitches are even. Pin the concave side to the convex side and, sewing away from the point (if there is one), sew on stay-stitching lines toward the center of the neck. Then sew away from the point toward the armhole. This will eliminate puckering at the points.

NOTE: You must always clip the point of the convex side of a yoke. This allows it to fit smoothly over the concave side.

RULE TO REMEMBER: To construct various yoke designs, draw design onto pattern, cut off, and add 3/8-inch seam allowance to both bodice and yoke.

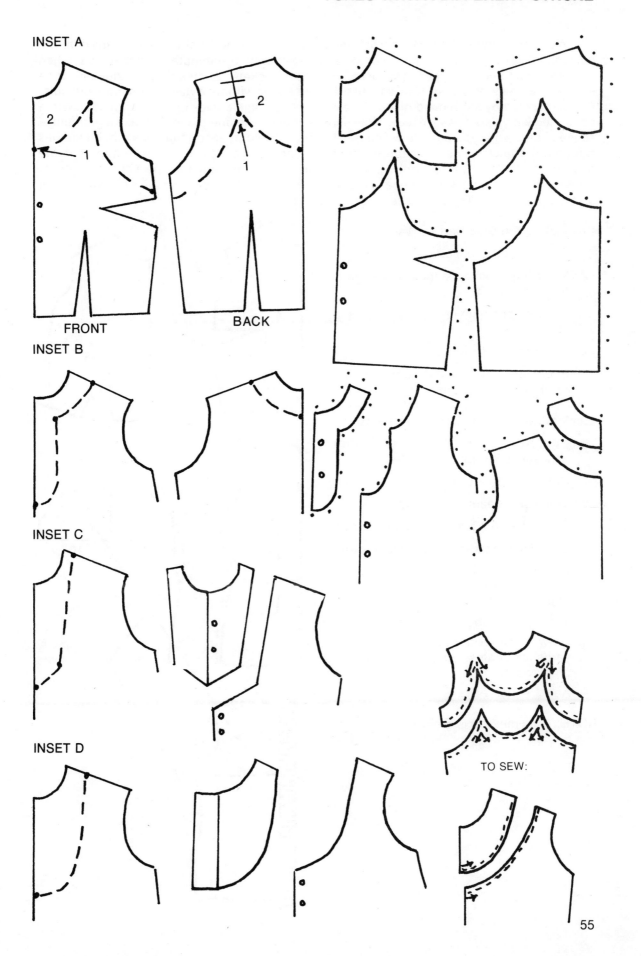

INSET A

FRONT   BACK

INSET B

INSET C

INSET D

TO SEW:

ELIMINATING DARTS

We have changed the dart control from one position to the other to create many different designs. There will be times, however, when you will want to eliminate the side dart, as when you are making certain types of blouses, dresses or jackets. Eliminating the side dart for a style with a waistline is easy. But what to do about a style without a waistline is more difficult. As you can see by the second diagram below, the waistline curves up to the outside. When combined with a skirt pattern (see "Waistless Wonder," the one-piece) to make a garment, a space is created at the outside waistline. In effect, the dart space that was eliminated has returned to the waistline. This throws the side seam from armhole to waist longer than the back to which it is sewn. The only successful way that I have found to cope with this problem is to use the bodice back as a guide and draw the front from this, curving the side front to give added bust space. Try it and see what you think.

Eliminating the Side Dart — Waist

1. Find dart control point.
2. Draw lines from waistline and side darts to control point.
3. Cut lines and pull side dart together and tape.
4. Eliminate protrusion at side.
5. Reconstruct waistline dart or use control in pleats or gathers.

Eliminating the Side Dart — Waistless

6. Construct a one-piece back from "Waistless Wonders" chapter.
7. Cut off for blouse if desired.
8. Trace side seam onto paper.
9. Curve the bust area as diagram shows.
10. Cut off a bodice front pattern as shown.
11. Place armhole (from Item #10) of bodice against side of drawing (Item #8).
12. Trace around bodice front section.
13. Draw in center front by placing yardstick against center neckline of drawing.
14. Add 1/4-inch ease.

NOTE: This method is great for sweater tops.

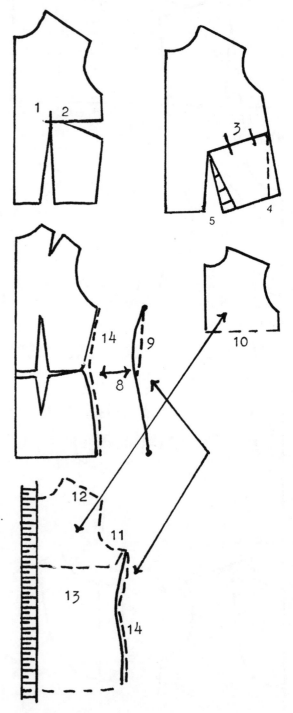

Collars have been around for a long time, and it isn't likely that they will disappear from the clothing scene. They add zest and personality to a garment. Collar styles vary from year to year but since they are all constructed from the basic collar cuts, you can construct your own once you determine what the basic cut is. And you can save your basic collar patterns to use over and over again.

When you are shopping and see a collar you like, examine it closely. Look first for the grain-line of the fabric. Once you establish this, you will be able to follow the grain line and determine how the collar was cut. Note the collar depth at the center back of the collar and also at the center front. I carry a six-inch piece of tape-measure in my pocketbook to use for measuring collars, pockets, etc. And remember, I advised you in the first chapter to always carry a notebook with you.

Although they come in many shapes and sizes, there are only five basic collar designs. All of the various shapes and forms of collars originate from these. In the following chapter, we will study thirty-two of these variations.

Below you see the five basic collar styles:

PETER PAN   SHIRT   MANDARIN

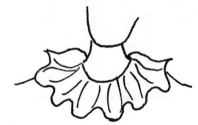
RUFFLE

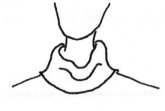
BIAS

COLLAR COLLECTION

STYLE #1 — PETER PAN: This collar has been around for a long time in one form or another. It dates back at least to the 1400's. The Ancient Egyptians used a form of this collar as neckwear. Since the Peter Pan follows the outline of the neck, it would likely be the first to be designed.

Pattern Construction:

1. It is very important in collar-making to follow every step. In the Peter Pan, you must overlap the outside shoulder area. If you fail to do this, your collar will not lay close to the garment but will protrude. Please follow the rules!

2. Lay bodice front and bodice back patterns with the necks touching and the armhole overlapping 1/2 inch. Tape.

3. Determine width of collar.

4. Use measuring tape to measure the width of the collar from the neck onto the bodice. Move tape and dot every 2 inches around the neck.

5. Sketch collar in.

6. Lay a piece of paper under neckline.

7. Draw 1/8 inch beyond neckline. This is very important. See sewing instructions.

8. Cut out collar pattern.

9. Use as is or round off as diagram shows.

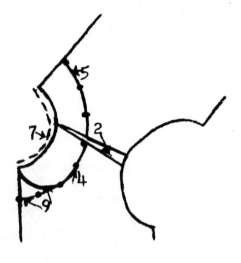

To Sew: Use interfacing that is not too firm. If fabric is used, make sure the center back of the interfacing is cut on the bias. This will give a good roll. Place interfacing to upper collar, stay-stitch, and attach facing. Sew the curve of the collar very shallow so that it will be nicely rounded when turned. See chapter on "The Finishing Touch" (Curves). Since you cut the neck of the collar smaller, you will have to stretch it by stay-stitching before sewing onto the neck. You must stretch the neckline as you stay-stitch. Apply to neck. This method makes the collar have a nice roll and eliminates puckering.

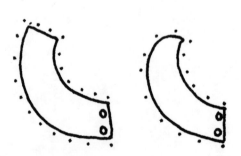

STYLE #2 — THE NAUTICAL COLLAR: This is one collar that is ageless. It never seems to go out of style, but will change its personality from time to time. The nautical collar originates from the Peter Pan collar.

Pattern Construction:

1. Lay a bodice front and back together at the shoulders with necklines touching and armholes overlapping 1/2 inch.

2. Determine the depth of your neckline in front. Dot.

3. Dot at shoulder 1/2 inch beyond shoulder. There is a certain amount of take-up in turning a collar and this eliminates a too-short collar.

4. Draw between dots. This line may be straight or curved. Presently the curved line is used.

5. Determine the depth of collar back. Dot.

6. Draw straight across. Intersect with line from shoulder.

7. Draw line for neckline from neckline dot to shoulder. This line may be straight or curved. Curved lines lend a softer look.

8. Cut away unused portion of neckline.

9. Lay paper under neckline and tape.

10. Extend neckline 1/8 inch, working gradually into front.

11. Cut out entire collar pattern.

To Sew: Interface collar. If decorative tape is used, sew to upper collar and interfacing before attaching to undercollar. Stretch neckline as you sew.

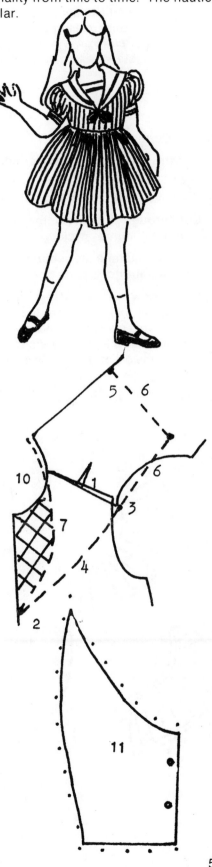

STYLE #3 — MODIFIED PETER PAN: The modified Peter Pan is a collar with a stand. In other words, it doesn't follow the lay of the dress. The stand may vary from just a little to *almost* a straight stand. A straight stand is a collar with the back of the collar making a double stand; the fold-over is equal to the stand. The modified Peter Pan is more feminine than the shirt collar but when used to the maximum stand, can give a tailored look.

Pattern Construction:

1. Construct a Peter Pan collar according to directions of Style #1.

2. Draw lines every inch around collar.

3. Cut through lines from the outside to within 1/4 inch of neckline.

4. Overlap and tape the sections to the desired amount of stand.

5. Make new collar pattern from this, *adding 1/2 inch* to the outside back of collar. This gives the collar some of the amount that is lost in the stand. *Add 1/8 inch* to inside of neckline for stretch.

To Sew: Follow directions for Peter Pan.

STYLE #4 — THE LAPEL COLLAR: This collar is in the family of the Peter Pan. It is used on lowered necklines and gives the effect of collar and lapel all-in-one.

Pattern Construction:

1. Determine collar design. We will use both a square and V-neckline for our diagrams.

2. Use two bodice front and back patterns — one for the collar and one for the bodice itself. Lay together and tape at **shoulders, overlapping 1/2 inch at armholes.**

3. Draw in neckline. Cut out of both patterns. Lay one aside.

4. Draw collar design. Cut out.

5. Additional stand can be obtained by slicing as you did for modified Peter Pan. See diagram.

To Sew: Stay-stitch neckline to prevent stretching. Sew as you would a Peter Pan.

COLLAR COLLECTION

STYLE #5 — THE PURITAN COLLAR: Just imagine a little girl all dressed up in a pretty little dress with a Puritan collar. This collar is used in round, pointed and square versions. We'll use the round version for demonstration.

Pattern Construction:

1. Tape bodice front and back patterns at the shoulders. *Do not overlap.*

2. Draw in design, extending shoulders 1/2 inch for take-up allowance.

3. Cut out pattern.

To Sew: This collar needs a firm interfacing so that it will hold its shape. Lay interfacing against upper collar. Stay-stitch, keeping seam even, along outside seam of collar. Pin undercollar to upper collar. Sew along stay-stitching. Trim seams; turn and press. If you are using lace or other trim, sew to upper collar on stay-stitching lines before attaching undercollar.

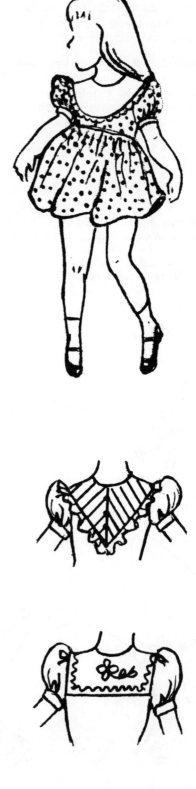

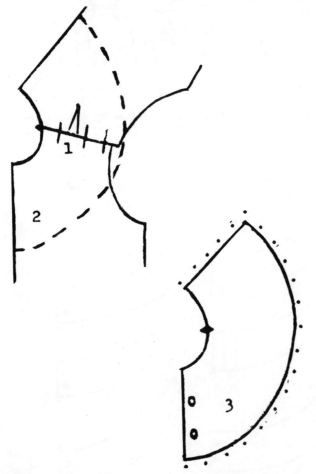

STYLE #6 — THE CAPE COLLAR: This collar is usually around in one form or another. It is very easy to sew up and the effect is beautiful.

Pattern Construction:

1. Place a bodice front and back against a straight edge with shoulders touching at neckline. Armhole will not meet.

2. Lay a large piece of paper under the bodices.

3. Draw design as diagram shows or think up one of your own.

To Sew: Bind the neckline. Finish off the outside edges with a roll hem or a decorative machine-stitch hem. You may also use lace or ruffle edging.

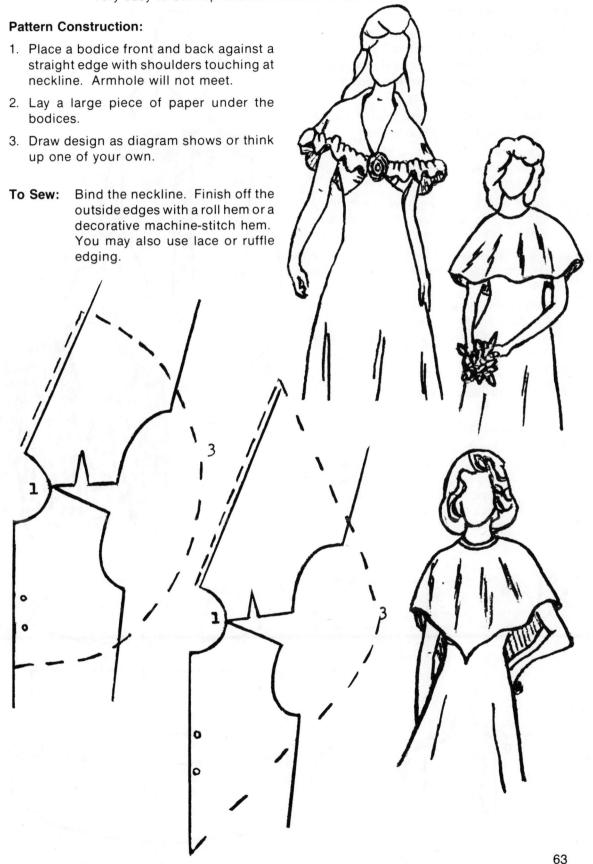

COLLAR COLLECTION

STYLE #7 — SHIRT COLLAR: The basic shirt collar is very easy to work with. The only thing that changes about this collar from year to year is the point of the collar, which will vary from a very short collar point to a very exaggerated point.

Pattern Construction:

1. Measure the neckline of your bodice front and back patterns. To do this, stand tape measure on its side and allow to fall with the curve of the neck. Measure twice for accuracy.

2. Multiply by two to get total neckline. Take off 1/4 inch (for stretch).

3. Draw this amount on a plain piece of paper. Make a dividing line at center. Dot each end.

4. Dot 1 to 1-1/2 inches down from line at center. This will determine collar stand. If collar depth is over 2 inches, use the maximum.

5. Determine collar depth at center back. Dot.

6. Determine depth and shape of point. In the diagram you see a round, short point and an exaggerated point. Dot. Draw in top of collar.

7. Draw in curve of stand.

8. Draw end lines to collar points or draw in curve for that version.

9. Cut out pattern.

To Sew: Use interfacing that is very firm if you wish your collar to have a very tailored look. Interface the upper collar. Stay-stitch collar neck (after collar has been completed), stretching as you sew.

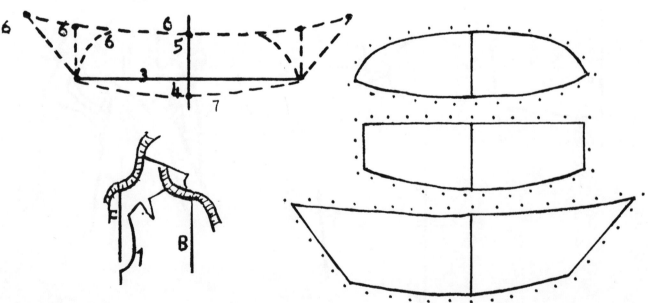

STYLE #7a THE SHAPED SHIRT COLLAR: There are some dresses and dressy suit jackets that need a more feminine collar than a shirt collar. The shirt collar is tailored and has a definite stand at the back of the neck. A modified Peter Pan is much more feminine but does not lend itself to a lapel. (If you have a garment with a Peter Pan collar, try to lay the neck open to simulate a lapel and you'll see what I mean.) So the answer is a collar combination. If we combine the shirt collar with the modified Peter Pan, we can achieve the effect we need.

Notice the difference in the rear-view diagrams below. See how the shaped shirt collar gives a softer appearance.

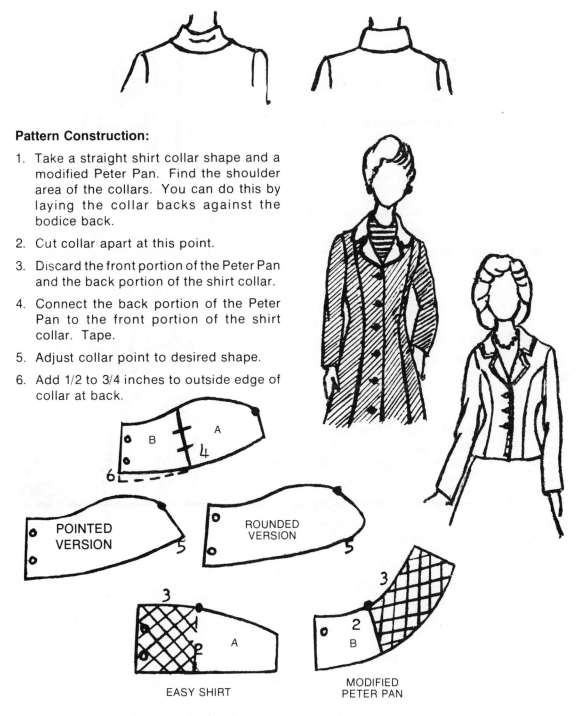

Pattern Construction:

1. Take a straight shirt collar shape and a modified Peter Pan. Find the shoulder area of the collars. You can do this by laying the collar backs against the bodice back.

2. Cut collar apart at this point.

3. Discard the front portion of the Peter Pan and the back portion of the shirt collar.

4. Connect the back portion of the Peter Pan to the front portion of the shirt collar. Tape.

5. Adjust collar point to desired shape.

6. Add 1/2 to 3/4 inches to outside edge of collar at back.

POINTED VERSION

ROUNDED VERSION

EASY SHIRT

MODIFIED PETER PAN

STYLE #8 — MANDARIN SHIRT COLLAR: This collar is very tailored and is used to create a definite stand. It is usually cut in two sections for men's shirts and very tailored women's shirts. However, it can be cut all in one piece. This gives a softer look and is easier to sew.

Pattern Construction:

1. Draw a vertical line on a piece of paper the depth you wish your collar back to be. In our diagram, I'm using 3-1/2 inches.

2. Divide your line and dot, giving 1/2 inch more to the upper portion. This will be the collar. The lower portion will be the mandarin.

3. Measure your bodice front and back neckline using measuring tape. Let's say 7-1/2 inches for our diagram.

4. Draw a line 7-1/2 inches from the dot on your vertical line.

5. Draw a parallel line from the bottom of your mandarin 7-1/2 inches. Connect these with a line.

6. Curve both of these lines from back of collar neck toward center front.

7. Add button extension. This depends upon the amount of extension you have allowed for your shirt.

8. Determine shape of collar point dot. Let's use a moderate point for our diagram with a 3-inch depth.

9. Draw line from back of collar to dot.

10. If collar is not to be separated, leave as is. To separate, cut on fold line.

To Sew: For separated collar, sew collar portion as you would a plain shirt collar. Place interfacing to the portion of the mandarin that will be exposed to the outside. Sew mandarin and facing to collar. Sew facing to neck first. Turn under mandarin (with interfacing) and top-stitch. To get a smooth finish, turn under and pin every inch before you top-stitch. It works best if you start pinning at center back, then fronts, and then shoulders. Work the other pins in between.

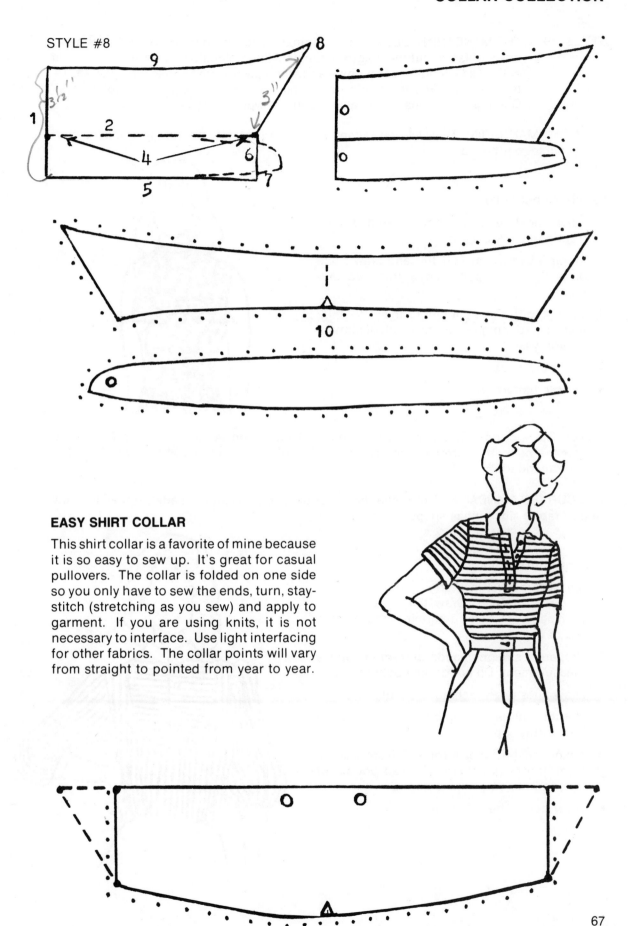

STYLE #8

EASY SHIRT COLLAR

This shirt collar is a favorite of mine because it is so easy to sew up. It's great for casual pullovers. The collar is folded on one side so you only have to sew the ends, turn, stay-stitch (stretching as you sew) and apply to garment. If you are using knits, it is not necessary to interface. Use light interfacing for other fabrics. The collar points will vary from straight to pointed from year to year.

COLLAR COLLECTION

STYLE #9 — THE MANDARIN COLLAR: The original mandarin collar was merely a straight piece of fabric cut the length of the neckline, folded over and sewn on. This collar had a tendency to wrinkle and stand away from the neck in an unattractive way. Cutting the fabric on the bias will aid in the way the collar lays. Curving the mandarin will also aid in the way this collar fits.

STRAIGHT MANDARIN: This style lends itself well to very soft fabrics with give. Our version is, of course, on the bias.

Pattern Construction:

1. Take neckline measurement from bodice front and back patterns.

2. Multiply by two, take off 1/4'' and draw a line on a piece of paper to equal this measurement.

3. Draw another line parallel to this 1 to 1-1/2 inches, depending upon the width of mandarin you wish.

4. Fill in the ends.

5. Double pattern.

NOTE: The width of a mandarin collar should depend upon the length of the neck. The shorter the neck, the narrower the mandarin. A very short neck might look better with a 3/4-inch mandarin.

THE CURVED MANDARIN: This collar has a lot of style and can be made from almost any type of fabric since it has shape.

Pattern Construction:

1. Measure neck 1 inch above shoulders. Add 1/2 inch for ease. Draw this measurement onto paper. This step determines the fit of the top of collar.

2. Prepare a straight mandarin from the above measurement. Do not double pattern.

3. Draw lines every inch across pattern.

4. Cut through lines from bottom to within 1/4 inch of the top.

5. Take neckline measurement from bodice front and back patterns. Spread bottom of mandarin to equal this amount.

6. Draw new pattern from this.

STRAIGHT MANDARIN

CURVED MANDARIN

LOWERED CURVED MANDARIN
See page 70

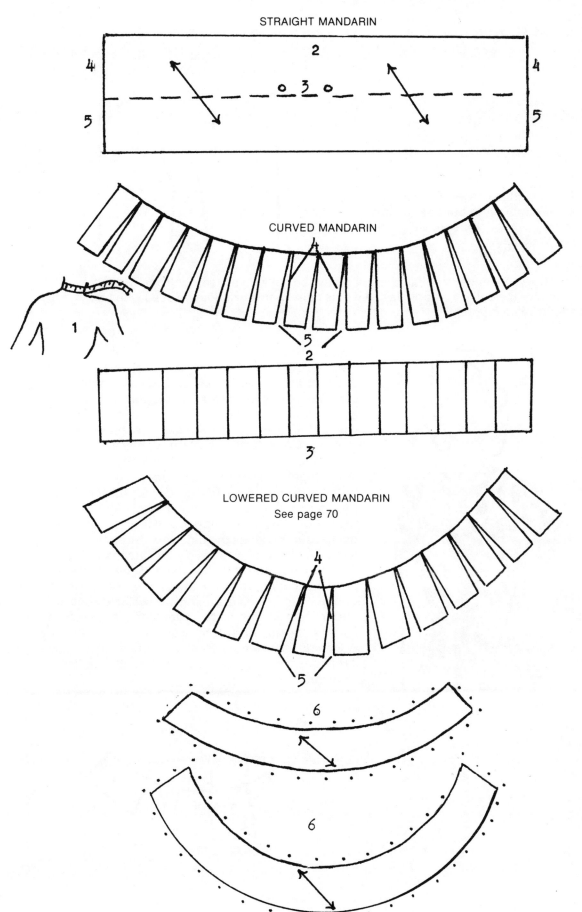

STYLE #9 (cont'd)

LOWERED CURVED MANDARIN: This mandarin has its advantage in that it does not ride as high on the neck and, therefore, does not constrict the neck as much. Try it and see if you like it.

Pattern Construction:

1. Take 1/4 inch off the neckline of the bodice front and back patterns.

2. Measure new neckline.

3. Make pattern from directions for the curved mandarin but use the new measurement. Refer to diagram on previous page.

NOTE: Curved mandarin collars should always be cut with the center front on the bias. This helps to give the collar a smooth lay. A whole collar pattern should be used when cutting the mandarin. See diagrams.

To Sew: A mandarin collar should always look even to be attractive. This means the collar should be the same measurement all the way around. If you bobble as you sew, the evidence can be seen and the collar will look uneven. It is not hard to achieve an even look. Cut interfacing with the center front on the bias. Attach to upper collar. Sew upper and under-collar together along the top edge. Turn and press. With measuring tape, measure every 2 inches from the top of the upper collar down. Mark as you measure. Stay-stitch (upper collar and interfacing) using your markings to guide you. Stretch the collar as you stitch. Check to see if your stitches look even. Correct if not. Use this stay-stitch to guide you as you sew the collar onto the neckline. To finish the undercollar: if you are using lightweight fabric, turn under seam and whip; if heavier fabric is used, finish edge with zigzag stitch. Secure to neckline by "stitching in a ditch" from the upper collar. See directions for "stitching in a ditch" in chapter on "Finishes."

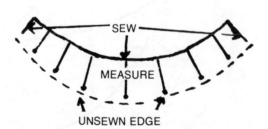

STYLE #10 — DRAPED COLLAR: This collar is very feminine and is best suited to soft fabrics. If you wish, you may use a firm fabric for your dress and a soft, sheer fabric for your collar, either in matching or corresponding fabric.

Pattern Construction:

1. Determine shape of neckline. Can be U or scooped.

2. Draw in your new neckline.

3. Measure neckline for both front and back. Multiply by two.

4. Lay out piece of paper.

5. Draw line on paper the length of the neckline measurement.

6. Determine depth of collar. Remember, this is a fold-over collar so your pattern will be doubled.

7. Make parallel lines the desired width on either side of first line.

8. If you want your collar to have an easy roll, add 1 inch to the collar length.

9. Add bias arrows to pattern.

To Sew: If you have added the extra inch, you will have to run easing stitch on seamline of completed collar. Ease as you would a sleeve. Fit to neckline. *Do not interface this collar.*

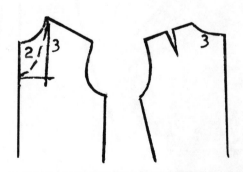

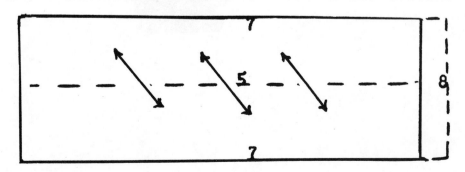

COLLAR COLLECTION

STYLE #11 — SHAWL COLLAR: There are many variations of the shawl collar and they are all beautiful and easy to sew. Hope you will want to try all the variations.

Pattern Construction:

1. Determine collar style from one of these variations or from one that you've seen in some shop, or on someone.

2. Take a bodice front and back and lay them as the diagram shows.

3. Determine width of collar back. Dot.

4. Determine where your first button will be. Dot. If you're not using buttons, determine where you wish collar to fold back.

5. Draw extension for the overlap.

6. Draw in collar, progressing from dot to dot.

7. At this point, the collar will lie down at the neck as does a Peter Pan. If you want the collar to have a stand, follow diagram. After slashing, rotate to desired stand.

To Sew: Sew collar together. See (A) in diagram. Sew bodice front and back shoulders together. Clip at (B). Sew neckline of collar to neckline of bodice back. Sew collar facing together at (C). Pin to collar of bodice (which is actually the undercollar). Sew from collar seam down to hem. Repeat for other side. That was easy, wasn't it?

STYLE #11

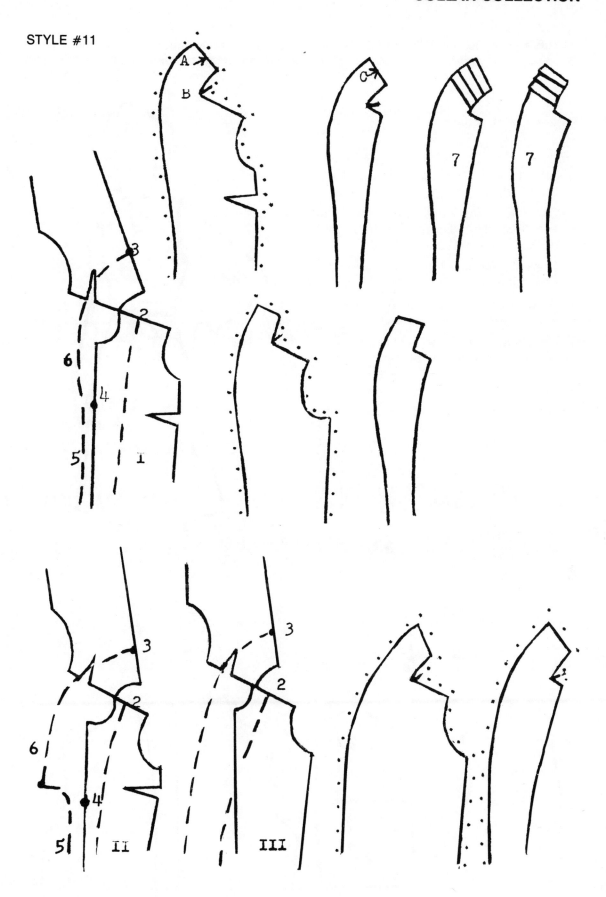

STYLE #12 — QUEEN ANNE COLLAR: As you can see by the illustrations, this collar gives a stand and at the same time gives freedom at the center front of the neck. This neckline is used on both tailored and dressy garments, and is flattering to most women.

Pattern Construction:

Version 1

1. Attach a piece of paper to neckline of both bodice front and back patterns.

2. Dot 1 to 1-1/2 inches above neck at shoulder, depending on length of your neck.

3. Draw sloping line from dot to shoulder on back and front.

4. Draw front neckline — then back neckline.

5. Move shoulder dart to neckline at back, which works much better with this design. Facing will not have this dart but should be cut on bias to give **stretch**.

To Sew: Pin interfacings to front and back bodices. Sew at shoulders. Sew facings at shoulder. Attach facing to dress and sew from center front out to eliminate puckering. Clip at point and turn.

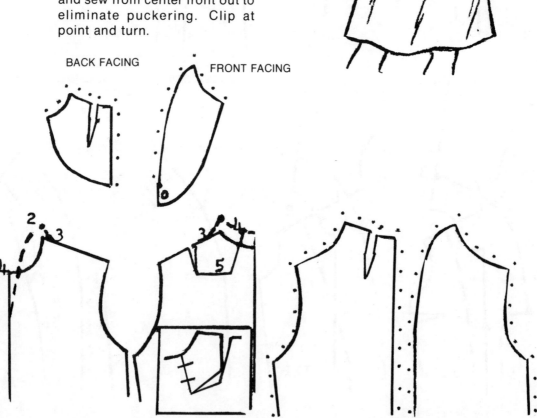

BACK FACING   FRONT FACING

STYLE #12 (cont'd)

Version 2

1. Lay back and front bodice with shoulders together. Tape.

2. Draw a parallel line 1-1/2 to 2 inches from shoulder on front bodice pattern.

3. Cut on line — separate.

4. Lay bodice front neck to back as you would for a shawl collar.

5. Determine depth of collar at back of neck — 1 to 1-1/2 inches.

6. Draw in new collar.

7. Draw slash lines and overlap to take out most of curve.

8. Change side dart to make shoulder gathers.

9. Make facing as diagram indicates.

To Sew: With this design, it works best to apply interfacing to facing. Sew facing and attached interfacing at neck back. Stay-stitch neckline of bodice. Gather at shoulders and sew to bodice back at shoulders. Attach facing and sew out from center front. Clip and turn. Sew facing to upper collar at back neck to secure.

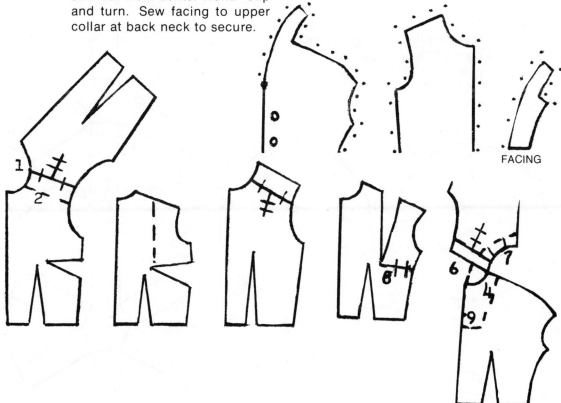

FACING

COLLAR COLLECTION

STYLE #13 — THE RUFFLE COLLAR: The ruffle collar first made its appearance as early as 1400. It was used on both men's and women's fashions. Today it is used to beautify and make a dress look really feminine. This collar can be gathered or rippled.

Pattern Construction:

Version 1 – RIPPLED COLLAR

1. Cut a strip of paper the length of your basic pattern neckline and the width you wish your collar to be.

2. Take off 1/2 inch as this collar stretches on the neckline edge. Divide into twelve sections.

3. Cut strip in half.

4. Cut both halves to within 1/4 inch of one edge.

5. Pull apart to form two circles.

6. Use these pattern circles to draw the collar onto the fabric.

7. Add 1/4-inch seam allowances to neckline edge and outside edge of circles. Cut across each circle.

8. One side of your cut will be the center back and the other side will be the center front. You may round off the front if you wish.

To Sew: Sew the center backs of both circles together. Finish outside edge by turning under and stitching with a decorative stitch. Sew to bodice neckline. Beautiful, isn't it?

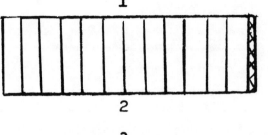

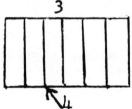

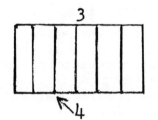

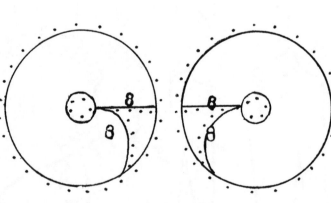

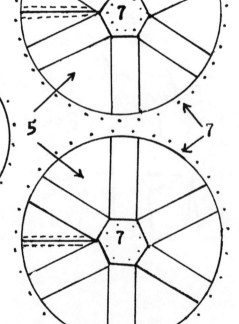

76

STYLE #13 (cont'd)

Version 2 – RIPPLED COLLAR (This is an easy method that I use.)

Pattern Construction:

1. Using a dinner plate (you read right), draw two circles onto your fabric.

2. Find the center of each circle.

3. **Draw a circle the size of your basic pattern neckline at the center of your two circles.**

4. Add seam allowance to neck edge of circles. Seam allowance for outside edge allowed in plate circumference.

5. Slice patterns on one side.

NOTE: A 10-inch plate will give you a collar approximately 3-1/2 inches wide when finished. To get a smaller width collar, use a serving bowl or a salad plate.

To Sew: Sew as for Version 1.

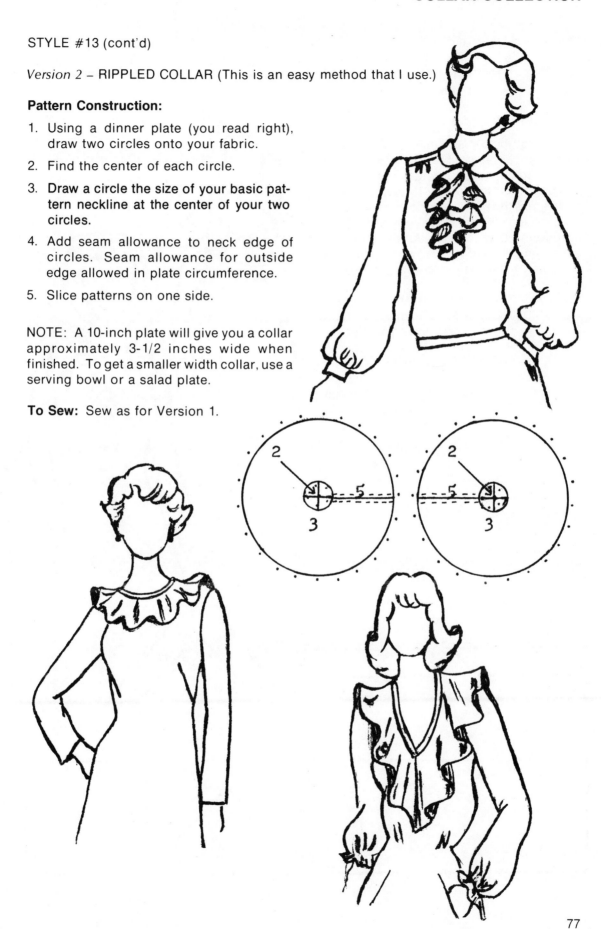

COLLAR COLLECTION

STYLE #13 (cont'd)

Version 3 – THE GATHERED RUFFLED COLLAR: This is a beautiful collar and lends itself well to either a round, square or V-neck.

Pattern Construction:

Cut bias strips of fabric the width you wish your collar to be and two to three times the basic bodice neckline measurement, depending upon the fabric. If fabric is sheer, three times the neckline is correct. You may have to piece the collar for your length, but I have found that you can work this into the gathers nicely and it won't show. See diagram below for the correct way to piece.

To Sew: If you had to piece the collar, sew these pieces together, being sure to press down your seams. Next, finish the outside edge of the collar with a decorative stitch on your machine. You may also finish the edge with a rolled hem if you like to do handwork (it takes a lot of time and patience). Gather to fit neckline and sew on. Pretty isn't it?

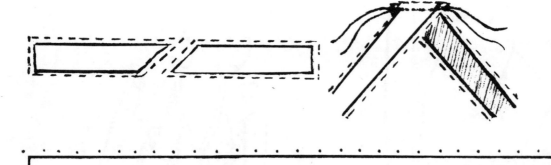

STYLE #13 (cont'd)

Version 4 – THE DRAPED RUFFLE: In the true sense, this is not a ruffle, but the same pattern is used for this design as is used for the ruffle collar. There is one difficulty in making this collar fit properly. As you can understand, the upper portion of this collar fits against the scooped neckline while the lower portion fits 4 to 5 inches below on the body. And as you move down the body from the neckline, it becomes larger. The secret of making this collar fit nicely is to ease the upper portion to make it smaller. As the collar is cut on the bias, this can be done easily since the ease is easy to work into a bias cut.

Pattern Construction:

Follow directions for making the ruffle collar, but you will not need to allow for gathering.

For Shirring: On one of the models, shirring is used every 4 to 5 inches. On the other, shirring is used only at the shoulders. Measure the neckline of the pattern, after scoop is determined. Cut drape to accommodate this area. At this point, set the collar aside and finish sewing your dress, including the neckline and facing. Take the collar drape and work around the neckline. Pin at the shoulders. Mark shoulder area on drape. Remove and sew easing stitch to the top portion. Fit on neckline again and pull easing stitch to fit the upper portion of the neckline. If you plan to do shirring every 4 to 5 inches, you will divide the neckline to determine exactly how far apart to make shirring stitches. Mark shirring areas on drape. Make shirring stitches as diagram shows, sewing one continuous stitching line starting at the bottom of the collar, moving to the top and, without cutting threads, turn and stitch down to the bottom. Pull bottom threads of both stitching lines at one time to make the shirring. The shirring will be worked in only at the shoulders for the loose drape. It's not necessary to hem this collar; just turn under 1/2 inch and tack at shirring areas.

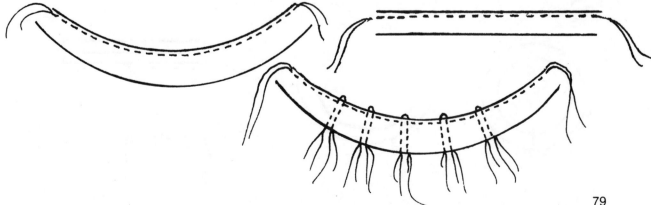

COLLAR COLLECTION

STYLE #14 — THE NECK BAND: Although neckbands are not really collars, I feel that they should be included with the collars because they do dress the neckline. Neckbands can be used from self fabric or commercial rib banding designed for neck and sleeves.

Version 1 – ROUND NECK BAND: This band can be used on lightweight pullovers as well as heavier sweater type knits. Just be sure your knit has plenty of stretch if you do not plan to use a neck zipper.

Pattern Construction:

1. Measure your basic pattern neckline. Double measurement.

2. Measure your neck 1 inch up from shoulder.

3. Determine width of band. We will use 1 inch for demonstration.

4. Cut strip of fabric on the crossgrain, double the band width and the length of your neck measurement. Add 1/4 inch seam allowances.

5. Sew the ends together if you do not plan to use a zipper at the back. Sew ends separately if zipper is used.

6. Sew folded band, stretching as you sew to form a curved shape. The bottom or seam edge will have to fit your bodice neckline measurement. The top or folded edge will fit your neck nicely.

7. Sew neckband to your bodice neckline. I find the center of my band and the center of the bodice front and back, and pin the band to those areas before sewing.

NOTE: If no zipper is being used, the seam of the band will look better if placed to a shoulder seam of the bodice.

If you desire a modified stand, take 1/4 to 1/2 inch off neckline before you measure.

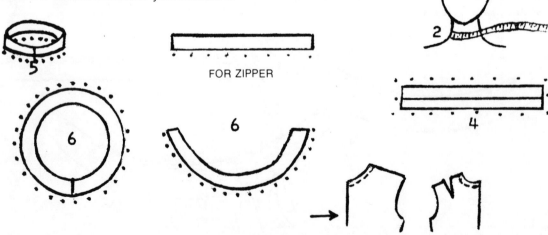

FOR ZIPPER

STYLE #14 (cont'd)

Version 2 – CARDIGAN BAND: This is one jacket that seldom goes out of style. Its personality will change and it's length will go up or down. This design is also one that is used in a tailored or dressy manner.

Pattern Construction:

1. Draw neckline on basic bodice. Take off 1/4 inch at shoulder.

2. Draw off 1/4 inch at the shoulder neck of basic pattern back. Taper to back of neck.

3. Cut away unneeded portions.

4. Measure neckline and front of jacket. Double measurement.

5. Cut a strip of fabric on the crossgrain the length of neckline measurement plus 2 inches and double the desired width, plus 1/4-inch seam allowances. If you have to piece to get the desired length, do it so that your seam will fall at center back.

6. Stay-stitch jacket neckline. Stay-stitch band with edges folded.

7. Pin to jacket starting at center back of neckline. Stretch more at back of neck and less down the front of the jacket. Sew from band side so that you can keep your band width even. See Version 1 for more complete details.

NOTE: When I stay-stitch the band, I use a ruler as a guide to keep the stitches exactly the same amount from the folded edge. Then it's a breeze when you sew to jacket.

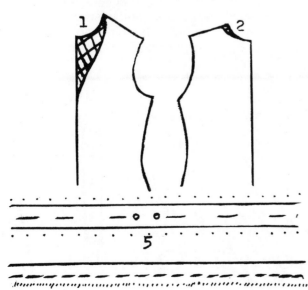

STYLE #14 (cont'd)

Version 3 – SET-IN NECKBAND: This version is different from the other neckbands in this chapter in that the pattern is shaped to follow the shape of the neckline. Therefore, because of the shaping, you may use any type of fabric without regard to its stretching qualities. This neckband can be used for dresses, shirts, and cardigans. We will do three versions for demonstration.

Pattern Construction:

1. Determine width of neckband. Let's use 1-1/2 inches for demonstration.

2. Draw neckline onto bodice front.

3. Measure 1-1/2 inches from edge of neckline with the exception of center front. Divide on either side of center front.

4. Repeat for bodice back if design follows back of neckline.

5. Cut out neckband.

6. Make facing for neckband.

7. Back of neckline can be taped to front. This will throw the seam to center back, which gives you only one seam to deal with.

8. Shirt collar type of set-in.

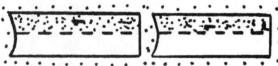

To Sew: (1) Cut interfacing for neckband. (2) Lay neckbands onto right side of bodice front, with interfacing next to center front. (3) Sew from bottom of band to neck. (4) Clip corners. (5) Turn bodice to wrong side. Fold evenly at position of neckband bottom. (6) Pull out unsewn ends of neckband sections and unsewn bodice portion. (7) Pin carefully. (8) Sew across ends. Folding the bodice evenly allows you to sew the bottom of the neckband straight. Apply collar. Use same technique for Style C.

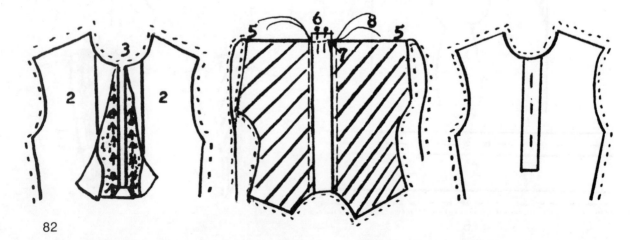

STYLE #14 — THE SET-IN NECKBAND

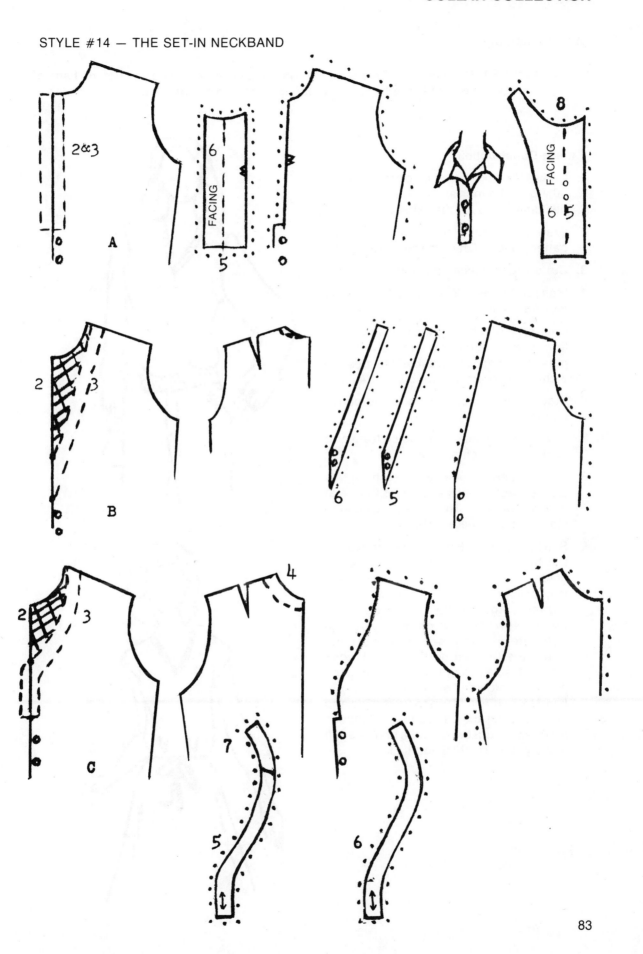

STYLE #14 (cont'd)

Version 4 – THE V-NECK BAND: This is my favorite for a pullover. Once you get the hang of sewing one of these bands, you can sew one on blindfolded.

Pattern Construction:

1. Draw a V-neckline on basic pattern front, taking off 1/4 inch at shoulder. A curved neckline gives a softer effect.

2. Draw off 1/4 inch of the neckline on basic pattern back. Graduate to center back.

3. Cut away unneeded portions.

4. Measure neckline of pattern. Double measurement.

5. Cut a strip of fabric on the crossgrain the length of the neckline measurement, plus 2 inches and double the desired width, plus seam allowances of 1/4 inch.

6. Stay-stitch neckband with folded edges together.

7. Sew shoulder seams of bodice front and back. Stay-stitch neckline.

8. Pin neckband to bodice. Stretch slightly on the front of neck and stretch more at the back of neck. This allows the band to stand close to neck in back.

9. Start sewing the band on the left side of the bodice front. Skip 1-1/2 inches at center front before you sew. Sew all the way around the neckline, down to the center point on the right side. Clip point. Now lay your garment out with right side up. Work the right side of band under the unsewn portion of left side. Work left side of band under this until the band lies nice and smooth. *Do not pin band to garment*. Turn to underside and finish sewing the band the 1-1/2 inches that was left unsewn. A little practice will make you perfect. Good luck!

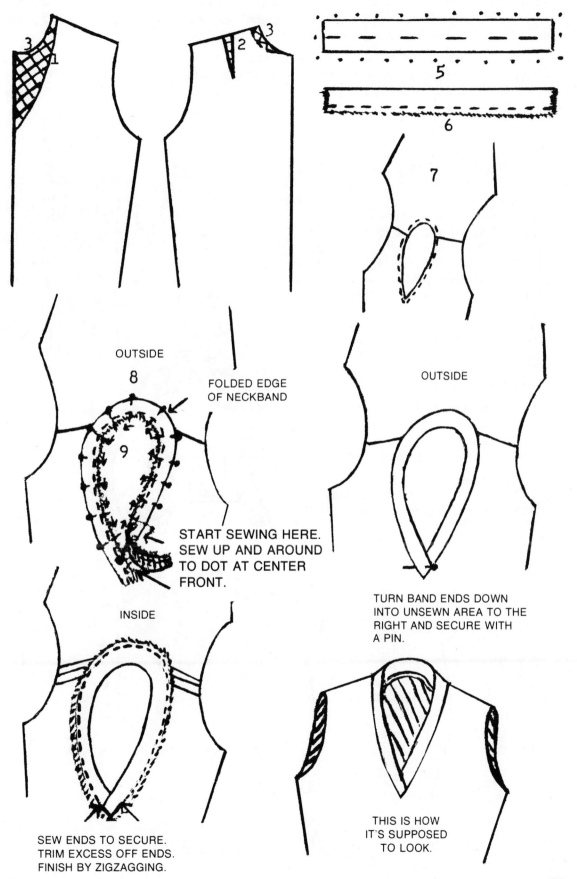

OUTSIDE

8

FOLDED EDGE
OF NECKBAND

9

OUTSIDE

START SEWING HERE.
SEW UP AND AROUND
TO DOT AT CENTER
FRONT.

TURN BAND ENDS DOWN
INTO UNSEWN AREA TO THE
RIGHT AND SECURE WITH
A PIN.

INSIDE

SEW ENDS TO SECURE.
TRIM EXCESS OFF ENDS.
FINISH BY ZIGZAGGING.

THIS IS HOW
IT'S SUPPOSED
TO LOOK.

COLLAR COLLECTION

STYLE #15 — LAPELS: Not to be confused with Style #4, the lapel collar. Although the lapel is not really a collar, it is usually associated with collars so it naturally seems the appropriate place to put them.

Lapels come in all shapes and sizes and the width of the lapel changes from season to season. They will fluctuate between very narrow to extremely wide.

Below are two versions for you to work on. There will be more in the "Jackets" chapter to give you further experience.

A. SHIRT LAPEL: The shirt lapel falls naturally when the collar is sewn onto the bodice. The overlap from buttonhole to the edge of the shirt front forms the lapel. The amount of overlap that you will use depends upon the size of your button. See "The Finishing Touch" chapter for proper overlap in relation to buttons.

B. WIDE SHIRT LAPEL: So termed because of extended size of lapel above first button.

Pattern Construction:

1. Determine size of buttons to be used on shirt or jacket. Draw their positions on the center front of bodice pattern. Attach a piece of paper for lapel extension.

2. Determine lapel width and draw in. If wide lapel is to be used, begin width extension in line with first button.

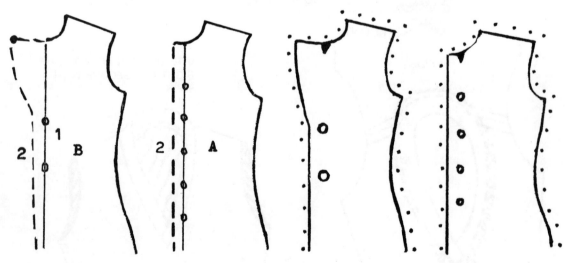

STYLE #15 (cont'd)

C. THE JACKET LAPEL

Pattern Construction:

1. Attach paper to front of bodice pattern.

2. Determine size and position of buttons to be used.

3. Determine the width you wish the lapel to be. This can be the same width as the collar front, wider or narrower. It can have a varied tip all the way from pointed to straight.

4. Draw in your button overlap.

5. Draw your lapel starting just above the first button.

6. Cut out.

7. Turn back at neckline to see how it looks. Maybe you want it to be wider or narrower, or maybe you didn't curve it enough. Whatever changes you want, you can make them now.

To Sew: Shaping is very important to the way a lapel will lie. I prefer to use two lightweight interfacings rather than one heavy. Attach interfacings to lapel and jacket. Sew lapel to jacket from tip of lapel down. To avoid a curved tip that often frustrates the seamstress, I have learned to sew off the tip approximately 1/4 inch by 1 inch. Try it! You'll be amazed at the results.

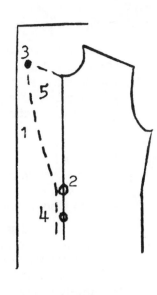

DO THIS

TO AVOID THIS

DRAPE TO SHAPE

THE COWL NECKLINE

The Cowl Neckline is one of the most flattering of all necklines. There are many variations of the cowl and there is one for you. If you wish to know how a cowl will look on you, take a scarf and fold into a triangle. Place the folded edge (which is on the bias) against your neck. Holding the ends, raise and lower to get different effects. Perhaps you'll like only one of the variations or you may want to use them all. The cowl is always cut on the bias to allow for better draping.

STYLE #1 — This cowl can be draped from a very small amount to a full drape. But any way you do it, it's beautiful.

Pattern Construction:

1. Use a folded scarf as directed below. To obtain the full drape, hold scarf to the neckline and let fall until the cleavage (3) is right. Hold scarf at points 1 and 2. Remove from neck and fold over, matching up 1 and 2.

2. Lay bodice pattern over folded scarf. Match neck at shoulder to points 1 and 2. Swing waist to meet fold of scarf.

3. Using this as an outline, draw a new pattern eliminating unneeded portions of the scarf.

4. If very lightweight fabric is being used, double the fabric just as you did the scarf. Fold again as you did in Step #2. Lay pattern on the center fold and cut. You will have a double front with the neckline on the fold.

To Sew: As bodice is cut on bias, you need to stay-stitch the seams to prevent stretching. Ease to fit bodice back.

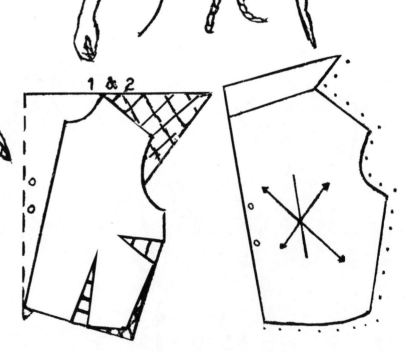

STYLE #2 — This is a very soft cowl and drapes rather loosely with no definite folds. It can be designed to lay on the neck with no fall or to fall loosely into a drape. This design can also be applied to a bodice back.

Pattern Construction:

1. Draw a V-shaped neckline on your pattern. This is to be determined by the amount of drape you wish. Use folded scarf to determine design.

2. Cut away excess.

3. Make three lines from center front to shoulder. These do not have to be precise.

4. Cut through lines, leaving 1/4 inch at shoulder.

5. Pull apart. The more you spread, the more drape.

6. Draw a line from waist to tip of first strip. Cut away excess.

7. Draw facing. It will be cut with the bodice and folded under.

To Sew: Follow directions in Style #1.

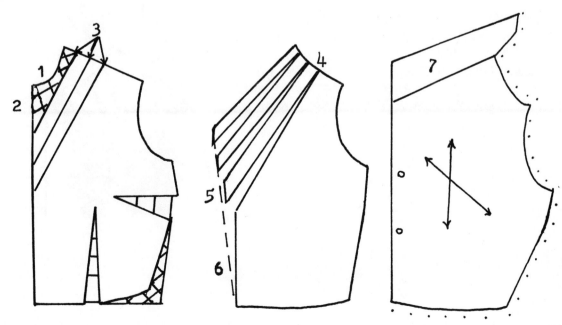

DRAPE TO SHAPE

STYLE #3 — THE INSET COWL: This cowl does not require the whole bodice to be cut on the bias. Only the inset portion will be on the bias. This cowl is especially lovely when different fabric is used for the inset. You might want to use a heavy fabric for the bodice, but use a matching sheer for the inset. Another way is to use a dotted, striped or check fabric as an inset.

Pattern Construction:

1. Determine shape of inset. This can be square, round or V-shaped. We will use a V-shape for directions.
2. Determine depth of V. Dot.
3. Determine width of V at shoulders. Dot.
4. Draw design.
5. Cut out. Use cut-out for cowl pattern.
6. Draw three lines on cut-out.
7. Cut through to within 1/4 inch at shoulder.
8. Pull apart to desired fullness. You might experiment with scarf.
9. Draw pattern and facing.
10. Double inset if lightweight fabric is used and eliminate facing.

STYLE #4 — INSET COWL WITH PLEATS: Pleats allow definite folds in the draping of the cowl.

Pattern Construction:

1. Follow above directions through Step 9.
2. Draw two lines on inset pattern from center to shoulder.
3. Separate completely, pulling apart 1-1/2 inches. Draw new pattern.

To Sew: Follow directions for sewing yokes from that chapter. To form pleats, fold toward center and stay-stitch on seam line.

STYLE #3

STYLE #4

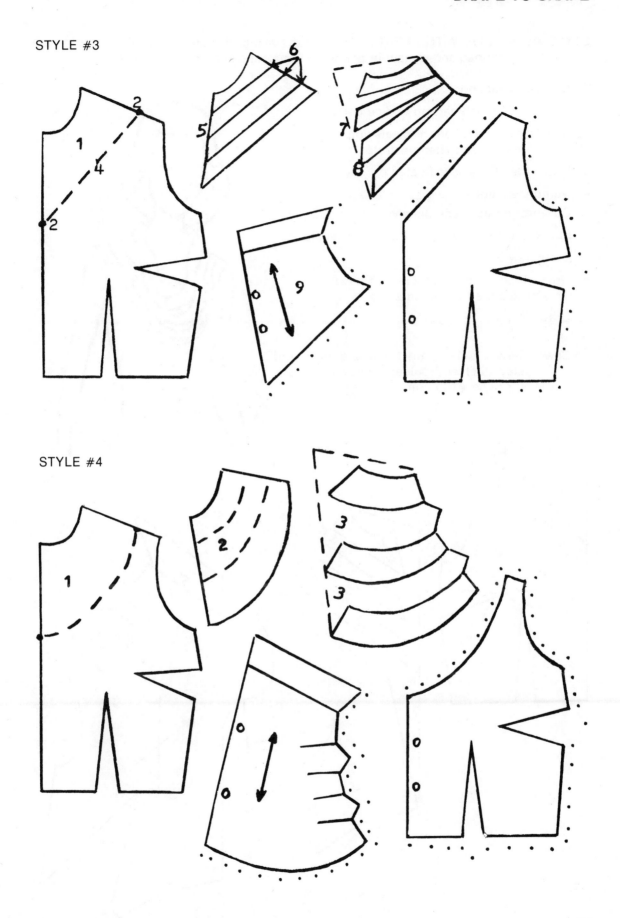

DRAPE TO SHAPE

STYLE #5 — COWL WITH PLEATS: The beauty of this design is that definite folds are formed and remain in place. You may use two or three pleats.

Pattern Construction:

1. Construct French dart on bodice pattern.

2. Determine the number of pleats you desire. We will use three to demonstrate.

3. Draw three lines as indicated on diagram.

4. Number sections.

5. Cut through lines completely.

6. Pull apart, allowing 2 to 3 inches for pleats.

7. Draw new pattern.

8. Draw stitching lines 2-1/2 inches down. This makes the folds lie in place.

9. Draw facing.

To Sew: Sew pleats. Fold toward center and stay-stitch at shoulder. Follow directions for Style #1 to complete.

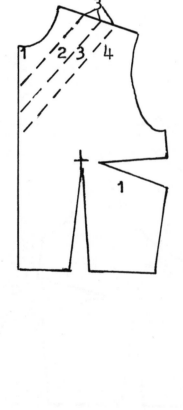

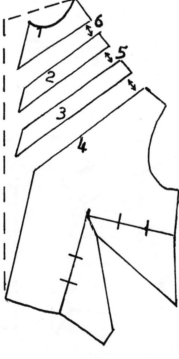

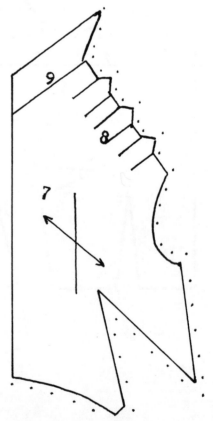

FACING FOR NECKLINE:

This facing pattern is for dresses with sleeves. Most patterns do not have adequate facings for dresses and, as a result, you have to whip the facings to secure them. This is a dead give-away of a home-made dress. Use deep facings as indicated in the diagram and you will only have to tack at shoulders, and you will have that custom look.

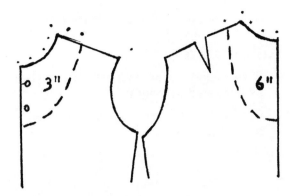

JACKET FACINGS:

There are a number of ways to face jackets. The drawings in the diagrams present the various ways for lined and unlined jackets. For unlined jackets, it is better to use more ample facings. This gives the jacket body a smooth, tailored look. You may choose to use a very lightweight lining and ample facing. In Figure B, the facing is extended 1 inch at the back of the neck. This is to be pleated into the neck. This, of course, is to give ease across the shoulders.

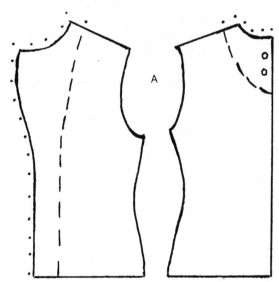

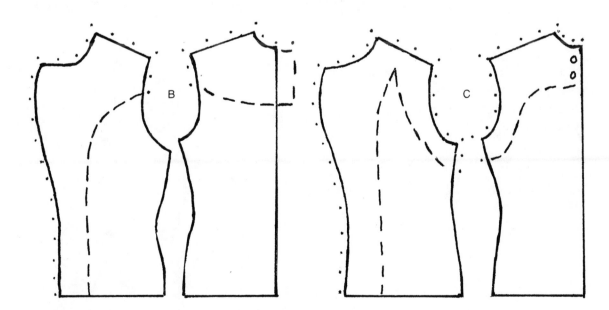

FACINGS THAT FIT

Facings are very important to a garment. If they do not fit properly, they will gape or pull. When you cut your facings from your own bodice pattern, they will fit properly and smoothly. You will be very pleased with the results.

FACING FOR SLEEVELESS DRESS:

1. Draw facing design for front and back bodice as indicated in diagram.

2. Cut away from your bodice pattern and use as facing pattern.

To Sew: (3) To eliminate the facing being exposed at the armhole or neck, you must cut the facing down at the armhole so that it will be smaller than the garment. Note diagram. (4) Sew shoulders of both the bodice and facing. (5) Lay right sides together. (6) Sew neck. (7) Sew armholes. (8) Pull through. Press.

NOTE: To use this method, you must have either the front or back of the bodice unsewn at center back or front. Otherwise, you would not be able to pull fabric through.

THE SCOOPED NECKLINE:

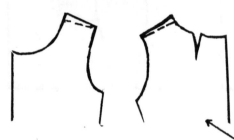

It is very simple to achieve various lowered necklines. *One important thing to remember!* The shoulder of your basic pattern is a slope. A woman's shoulders just do not slope straight but generally have a soft, curved slope which straightens only a couple of inches before the shoulder/arm area. When you scoop a neckline, you must straighten the shoulder of your pattern to eliminate poor fit. This method will give a smooth fit both at the shoulders and neckline.

Drawing the scoop:

1. Determine how low and how wide you wish the scoop. Dot.

2. Draw a square from the dots.

3. Sketch in scoop.

4. Remove unneeded portion.

Facing for scoop: Follow directions for sleveless dress.

FACING FOR SLEEVELESS DRESS:

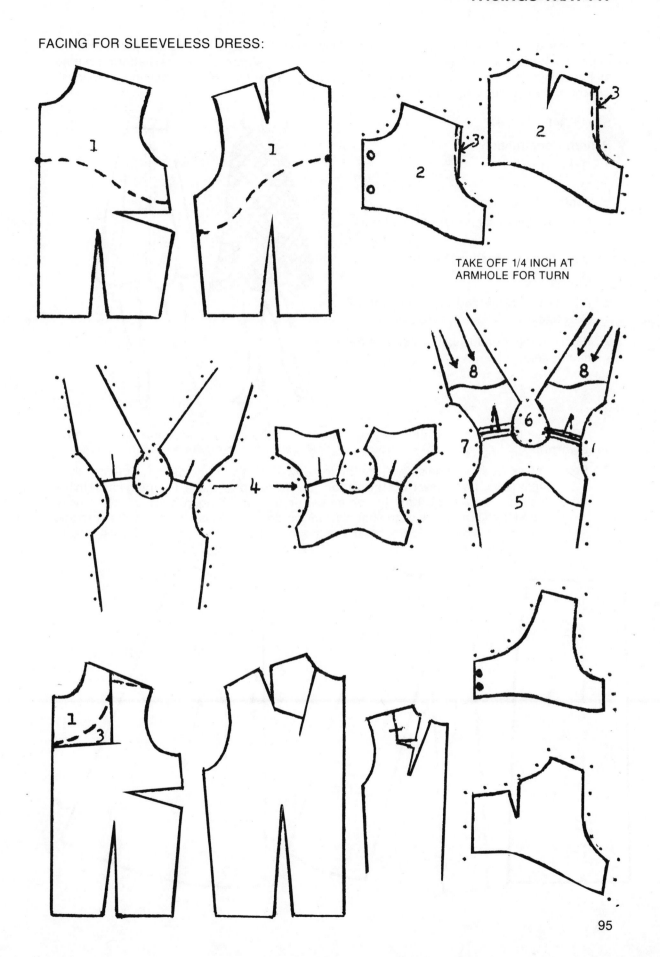

TAKE OFF 1/4 INCH AT
ARMHOLE FOR TURN

THE VERSATILE SKIRT

Skirts are a must for any wardrobe. They can be dressy or casual. But the most important thing is to find the most flattering style on you. I suppose the most flattering skirt to all figures is the simple A-line, but I wouldn't want you to get hung up on making all A-lines. Try them all and see what you think looks well on you!

STYLE #1 — A-LINE

Pattern Construction:

1. Dot dart point.

2. Measure distance from control point to center of skirt. Dot.

3. Measure this distance at bottom of skirt. Dot.

4. Draw line intersecting the dots.

5. Cut on line.

6. Pull dart together and tape. Repeat for skirt back.

7. Place on fold or add seam allowance for center seam.

That's all there is to it. Isn't it easy? You will have the best-fitting A-line skirt you have ever worn.

To Sew: All skirts should be sewn from the top down. This will ride out any pull the fabric may have. If you sew from the bottom up, you will often get a drooping effect in the fabric. Very important to remember in top-stitching a skirt panel: *Always* top-stitch both sides of the panel from top down. This is not as easy as stitching down one side and up the other, but the results of stitching properly will be worth the effort. Try it!

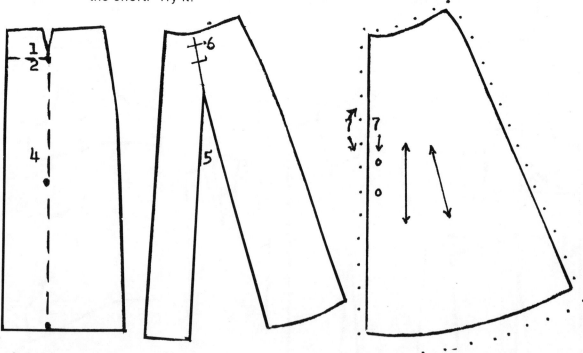

96

STYLE #2 — A-LINE WITH PLEAT: Very attractive; gives same easy fit as the A-line but with added interest.

Pattern Construction:

1. Follow directions for A-line skirt.

2. *If you are using 60-inch fabric:*
   Determine pleat depth: 4 inches will give a pleat with a depth of 2 inches. This really lays well. Lay your A-line pattern 4 inches away from fold of fabric.

3. *For 45-inch fabric:*
   You may have to add a pleat facing when using 45-inch fabric. To do so, cut a strip of fabric 4 inches plus seam allowance and the length of your skirt. Place A-line pattern 2 inches (plus seam allowances) away from selvage.

To Sew: *To sew pleat for 60-inch fabric:*
Fold pleats in place and top-stitch on either side. Trim excess around stitches if fabric is heavy.

To sew pleat with facing:
Sew facing to skirt, leaving twice the amount of hem unsewn at bottom. When you turn your hem, it is much easier to sew if you do not have the bulky seams of the facing to have to handle. After you hem the skirt, sew the facing at hem to the skirt. This makes the pleat lay well. Follow directions for 60-inch fabric to sew the pleat down at the top.

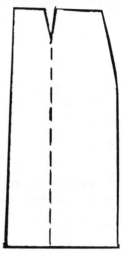

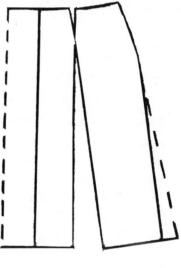

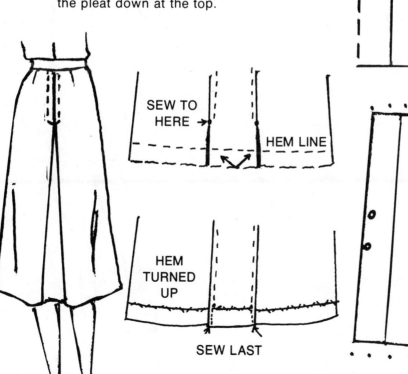

SEW TO HERE

HEM LINE

HEM TURNED UP

SEW LAST

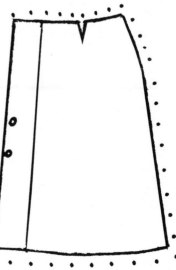

THE VERSATILE SKIRT

STYLE #3 — SIX-GORE: Six-gore skirts can vary from straight to a full swing at the bottom. Very flattering and very slimming.

STRAIGHT SIX-GORE:

Pattern Construction:

1. Find straight of grain for right side of skirt.

2. Dot dart control point.

3. Measure distance from dart control point to the center of skirt. Dot.

4. Measure this same distance from center front at bottom of skirt. Dot.

5. Cut on line. Separate.

6. Draw new pattern.

7. Place center front on fold.

8. Repeat for skirt back.

FLARED SIX-GORE:

Pattern Construction:

1. Follow directions for straight six-gore.

2. Determine amount of flare. Dot.

3. Determine point at which you wish flare to start. This can by anywhere from dart point to upper thighs.

4. Sketch flare. If much fullness is used, flare will be slightly curved.

5. Center of each panel and sides of each panel should have equal amount of fullness.

STRAIGHT SIX-GORE

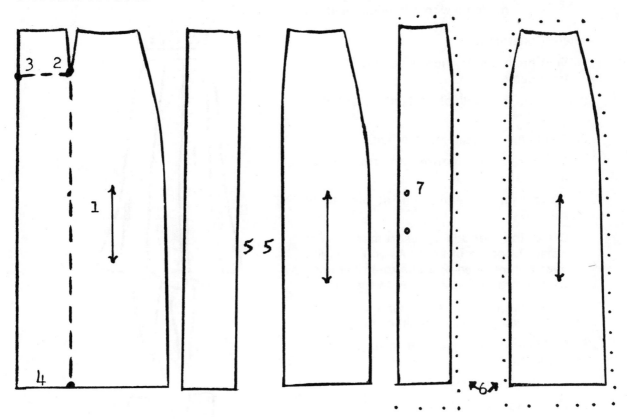

FLARED SIX-GORE   ## FLOUNCED SIX-GORE

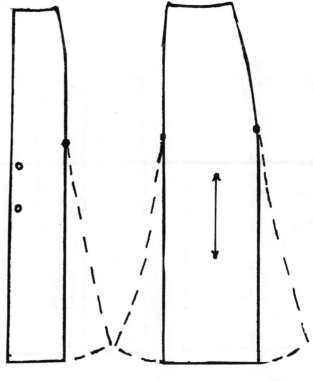

THE VERSATILE SKIRT

STYLE #4 — EIGHT-GORE: The eight-gore skirt is considered dressy, especially when made up with a flounced hemline.

Pattern Construction:

1. Find grain line for right side and 2 inches from center.

2. Measure the width of skirt pattern at fullest part of hip.

3. Divide this measurement in half.

4. Measure from center to the above measurement. Dot.

5. Make same measurement at bottom of skirt. Dot.

6. Draw line through measurements from waist to bottom of skirt. As you see, you have not included dart control in the line. Dart control must be moved to the line.

7. Fill in dart control. Apply same amount to line, dividing equally on either side.

8. Cut line, cutting the dart in as you cut. Separate.

9. Add desired fullness to all sides.

10. Repeat for back.

11. Flounced eight-gore is flared at thighs.

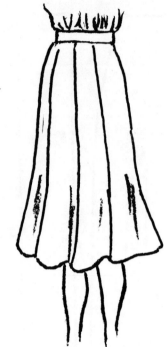

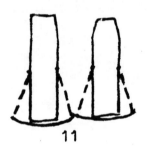

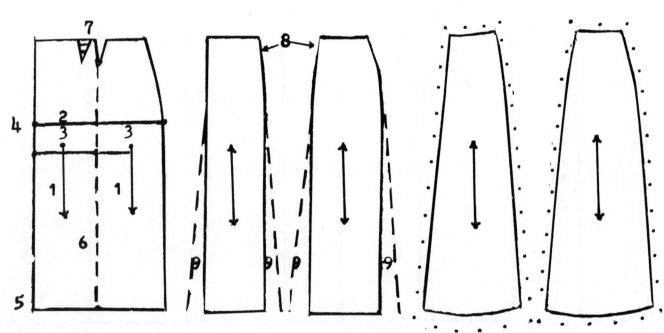

STYLE #5 — STRAIGHT SKIRT WITH SET-IN PLEATS: This is treated as an inset. You are to determine how much inset you wish and draw in both the front and back skirts. Tape skirts together at bottom of patterns and cut out inset.

Draw pleats on inset. Cut and pull apart to allow double distance between pleats.

To Sew: Fold front pleats toward center. Repeat with back pleats. Stay-stitch on seam line. Sew into skirt as you would an inset, *after* you have sewn your side seams together.

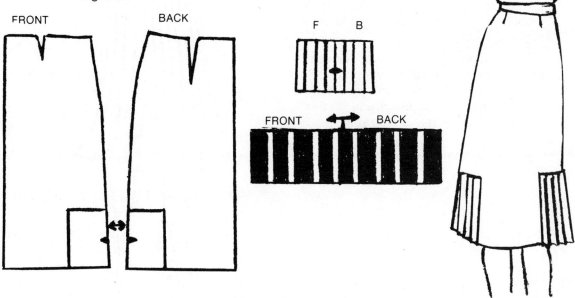

STYLE #6 — DOUBLE BOX PLEATS: 1. Separate at dart control. 2. Add 2-inch pleat extension from dart control to hem. 3. Make pleat inset. 4. Take off dart control. 5. Sew in darts. 6. Sew inset to pleats from arrows down. You may either whip top of inset to waist or top-stitch on either side of dart control.

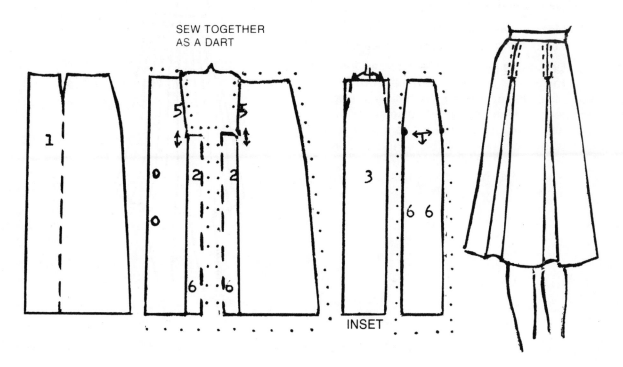

THE VERSATILE SKIRT

STYLE #7 — PLEATED SKIRT: The pleated skirt is in and out of fashion from season to season. They are always a nice change from the other styles.

UNSEWN PLEATS

Pattern Construction:

1. Measure waist.

2. Decide your pleat size. Let's say you plan 1-inch pleats and your waist is 26 inches. You will have 26 pleats to work into the waist.

3. Allow 2 inches to turn under for each pleat. You will need to cut your fabric 78 inches wide and skirt length plus hem. Since fabric is not wide enough for this, you will need to have a side seam.

To Sew: Since there is a certain amount of take-up room in fabric when making pleats, I begin making my pleats from each end and working toward the center. This way you can rearrange several of the center pleats to make your pleats come out right.

STITCHED PLEATS

Pattern Construction:

1. Measure your hip at the area you plan to stitch down to. Measure your waist.

2. Determine pleat width — let's say 1 inch for pleats. If your hips measure 38 inches at 7 inches down (which is average length of stitched-down pleats) you will need 114 inches of fabric for pleats and turn-under. We will divide this by two so that you will have a pattern for back and front. You have 57 inches plus skirt length.

STYLE #7 (cont'd)

STITCHED PLEATS (cont'd)

3. Take two strips of paper 57 inches wide, plus 1 inch for side seams, and the length of skirt. Since half of hip measurement is 19 inches and pleats are 1 inch, you will mark off pleat spaces as diagram below indicates.

4. If waist measures 28 inches and you divide by two, you will have 14 inches to cope with at waist on each pattern. Each pleat will be treated as a dart from the hip up. To get the amount to use in each pleat at waist, divide 14 by 19 which equals .74. Round it off to 3/4 inches since a little ease is needed.

5. Since each pleat will measure 3/4 inches at waistline, you will have 1/4 inch remaining of the 1-inch pleat allowance to incorporate into the dart (which will be the inside of the pleat). Divide and use 1/8 inches on each side of pleat. This will give a lot of bulk under the pleats, so you may want to trim excess when you have completed the sewing.

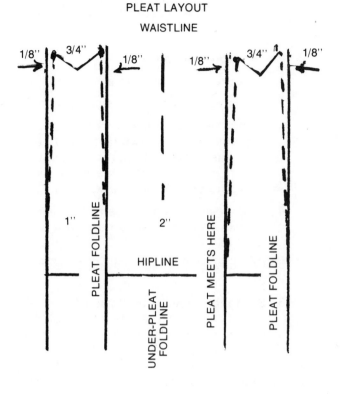

PLEAT LAYOUT

WAISTLINE

To Sew: In cutting out the skirt, you should mark all the darts from waist to hip. Fold the darts together and stitch either from the wrong or right side of skirt. If stitched from right side, you will top-stitch close to edge of pleat. If you are working with plaids, it is much easier to top-stitch the pleats. You can match the plaids as you sew. Make sure that the seams at each side are securely hidden under the pleats.

NOTE: In planning the pleat layout, use one-half of the under-pleat allowance (1 inch) on the ends of each pattern section. In sewing the skirt sections together, the side seams will fall in the center of the under-pleat, which will give a smooth finish.

CUT TWO

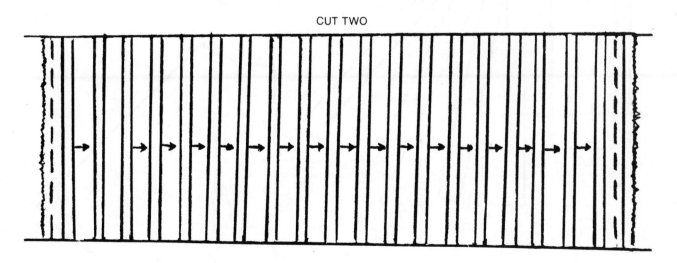

THE VERSATILE SKIRT

STYLE #8 — CIRCULAR SKIRT: After much experience working with various methods of creating the circular skirt, I find that the method below is the easiest and makes the most sense of any. You can also use this method for making a round tablecloth.

Pattern Construction:

1. Measure your waist and skirt length.

2. Divide your waist measurement by four.

3. Using this measurement, cut two paper patterns. You have two rectangles: the 1/4 measurement of your waist and the length measurement. One is for skirt front and one for skirt back.

4. Fold these rectangle patterns in half and then in half again. You now have four folds in each.

5. Cut through the folds, leaving 1/4 inch at top.

6. Swing the sections until you get the desired fullness. To get the true full circle, you must swing the sections to a 90-degree angle.

To Sew: Stitch side seams, leaving zipper space. Sew in zipper. Staystitch waistline and ease to fit waistband.

CUT TWO

FOLD

5 6

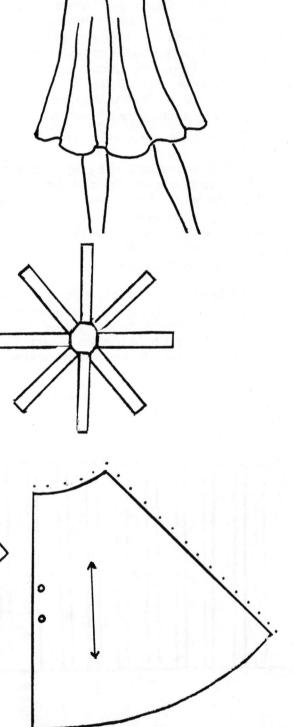

STYLE #9 — THE GATHERED SKIRT: Can be cut on the straight or on the A-line. Cutting on the A-line enables you to have fewer gathers at the waist, which eliminates bulkiness. This is slimming and it also has a pretty swing.

Pattern Construction:

STRAIGHT GATHERED SKIRT

1. Use anywhere from 1-1/2 to 3 times your waist measurement, depending on fabric weight and fullness you wish. Fabrics such as voile or silk can use 3 times the waist measurement.

2. Cut fabric the length plus hem, and the waist plus fullness. You may be able to do this from one width of fabric. If not, divide and give half to front and back.

A-LINE GATHERED SKIRT

1. Determine fullness desired.

2. Lay A-line pattern on fabric that has been folded. Allow enough fullness at fold for gathering.

3. If side seam is too curved, it may bulge after gathering. If so, sew out.

A-LINE WITH CENTER GATHERS

Follow directions for A-line gathered skirt, but allow only enough fullness for the front and back center.

To Sew: Always sew two gathering stitches 3/8 inches apart. Pull to fit waist. The double-stitching gives a smooth finish under the skirt band and also makes sewing onto band easier.

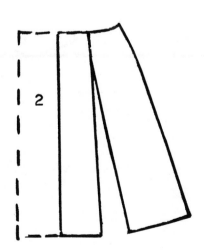

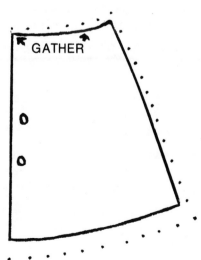

THE VERSATILE SKIRT

STYLE #10 — DIRNDL SKIRT: A Dirndl skirt has fullness at the top in the form of pleats or gathers but is narrow at the bottom.

Pattern Construction:

1. Dot skirt pattern twice at waist. Fill in waist dart.

2. Draw through to within 1/4 inch at bottom.

3. Cut on lines, leaving 1/4 inch at bottom.

4. Pull top of pattern apart to desired width.

5. This fullness can either be used for soft folds or gathers. If you use folds, they may be turned either toward or away from center.

STYLE #11 — YOKE SKIRT: The yoke is used on the skirt to take the place of the traditional waistband. Gives a nice fit and does not bind the waist.

Pattern Construction:

1. Draw yoke on skirt pattern back and front.

2. Tape darts together.

3. Cut yokes out.

4. Tape at sides.

5. As you can see, this yoke is cut all-in-one. It throws the back on the bias, which gives a nice fit over the hips.

6. You may change the dart control in the lower skirt back to the center.

7. Skirt may be A-lined if desired.

To Sew: Use a lightweight interfacing against the yoke. You must face the yoke also. If the material is very heavy, you may choose to use a facing of same color but lighter weight. Sew as for insets.

STYLE #10

STYLE #11

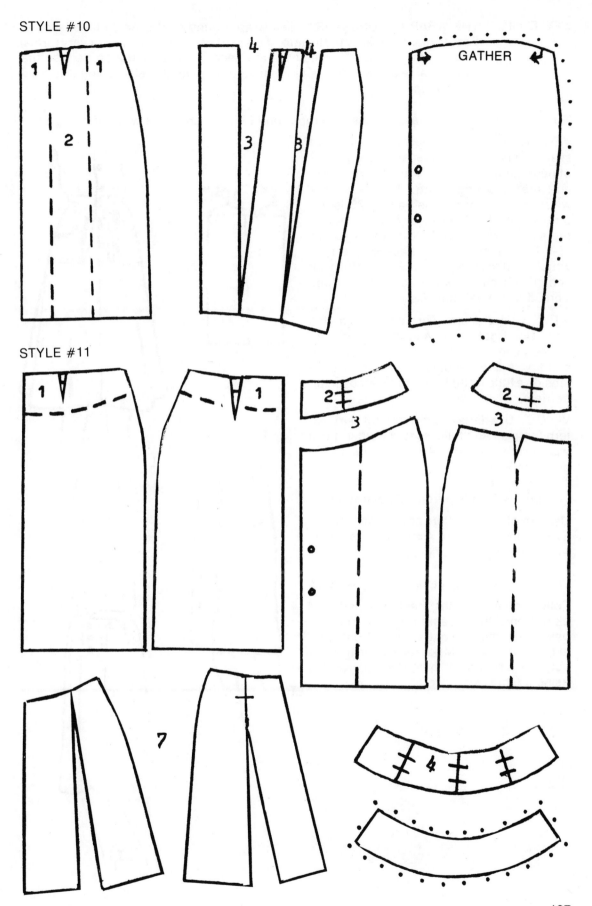

THE VERSATILE SKIRT

STYLE #12 — THE WRAP-AROUND SKIRT: The wrap-around skirt is an all-time favorite. Easy to make and easy to slip into. This skirt can be very casual or very formal, from denim to satin. Three styles are used for demonstration here so that you'll be able to have the basics for anything you might see that you would like to work up.

Version 1 – The all-time favorite casual wrap-around. There are three ways of doing this.

VIEW A: This style does not have side seams. It is cut in two pieces. Take a piece of newspaper the length you wish your skirt and the following width: Let's say your waist is 28 inches. One-half of 28 is 14; one-half of 14 is 7 — use for front portion of the skirt. Now, three-fourths of 14 equals 10-1/2. Use this for the back of the skirt which will overlap. Draw line through center and cut to within 1/4 inch of top. Spread to desired fullness.

VIEW B: Use A-line skirt pattern for this one. Use front as is. Add extension from above example (10-1/2) to the back skirt pattern. A-line the outside edge of the extension a little so that it will fit nicely over the derriere.

VIEW C: Use darts and the straight skirt pattern for this. Add fullness to the sides if you wish — see diagram. Add extension as example in View B.

Version 2 – This is a front wrap-around.

Use straight skirt pattern as diagram shows. Extension will be cut straight at opening. Add fullness to side if desired.

Version 3 – A dressy gathered wrap-around.

Follow directions for making a gathered skirt. Complete as diagram shows. You may use either the straight or A-line gathered skirt for this one. Make facing for front or you can turn a small hem under if you are using a fabric with give.

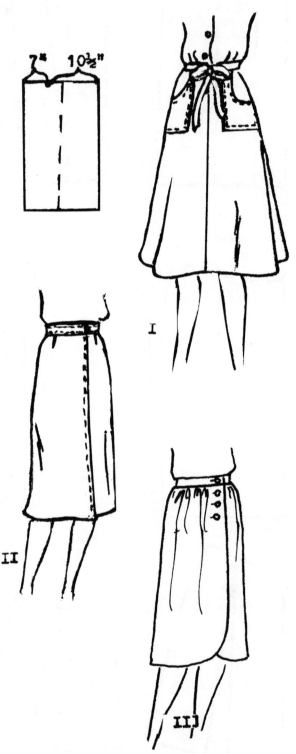

VERSION 1

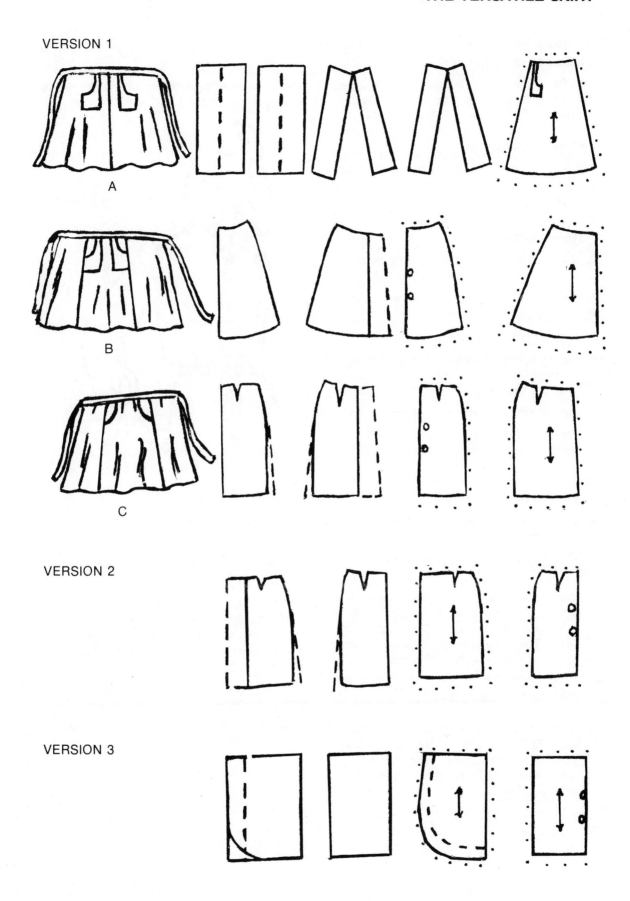

A

B

C

VERSION 2

VERSION 3

SHIRTWAIST

The shirtwaist dress can be starkly tailored or soft and feminine. It is one style that can be adapted to any situation.

The style shown below is very tailored. However, it can be made to look feminine by using fabrics such as satin or silk. It's good to have at least one tailored shirtdress in your wardrobe.

Pattern Construction:

1. Draw yoke on pattern back, allowing 3 to 4 inches from center neck. Cut on line. Separate.

2. Remove shoulder dart as directions below show.

3. Tape back yoke to pattern bodice front. Mark shoulders.

4. Draw 1-1/2 to 2-1/2 inches from shoulder, parallel with the shoulder.

5. Cut on line. Separate.

6. Add facing to center front, allowing enough for button extension. See *Facing* on opposite page.

7. Add 1 inch to bodice back for pleat.

8. Make fly front by directions below.

TO REMOVE SHOULDER DART:

A. Draw line from end of dart to edge of yoke.

B. Cut and pull dart together and tape.

C. As you can see, you have thrown your dart control to the bottom edge of the yoke. You have also created space which throws the bottom of the yoke too wide. The yoke does not look well unless it is straight, so we will take the dart control and move it to the *top of the remaining bottom section*. It doesn't show here but gives a good fit.

D. To cope with the space, cut off an equal amount at the side of the yoke. Draw yoke straight to compensate for the uneven edge made by the dart control. Now everything is back to normal.

TO MAKE FLY FRONT:

E. Determine fly width.

F. Cut piece of fabric width of fly plus 1/2-inch seams.

G. Cut interfacing width of the fly (no seams).

H. Press the fabric fly over the interfacing, placing interfacing in center and overlapping the seams on each side.

I. Pin fly to bodice front, matching center of fly to center front of bodice.

J. Top-stitch on each side. Sew downward on both sides to prevent puckering.

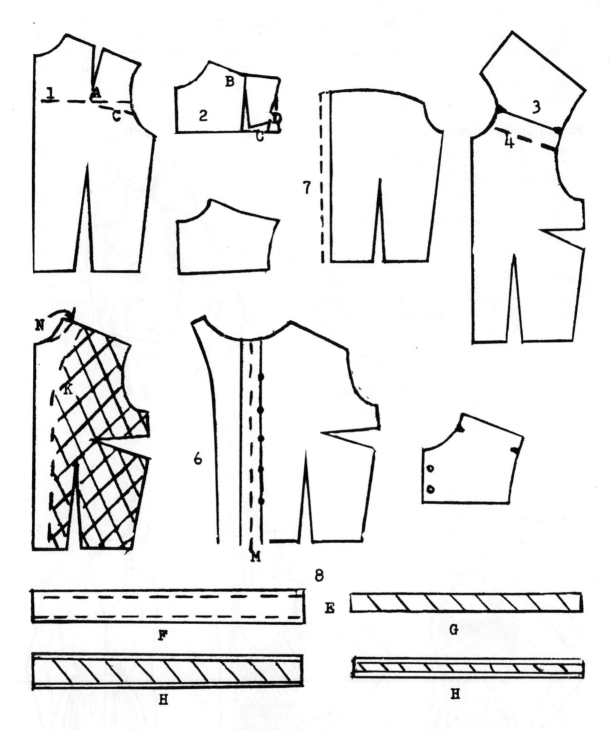

TO MAKE FACING:

K. Draw facing onto a bodice front pattern.

L. Cut off.

M. Place center front of facing against center front of front pattern, leaving room for button extension.

VERY IMPORTANT LESSON:

N. One of my students asked me to please stress the importance of this step: Shallow out the neckline of the facing. I have found that when you do this, it forces the facing to become stretched when sewn on and makes the facing lie smoothly. Otherwise, you will often have unsightly, loose bulges.

SUN DRESSES AND HALTERS

In the warm, sunny days of summer, one just has to find ways to keep cool. Sun dresses provide a way to beat the heat. Dress them up or down. They will go with you anywhere. Look at the versions below — don't they make you want to get your teeth into making a sundress?

Pattern Construction:

1. Draw design onto pattern bodices.

2. Cut off unneeded portions.

3. Cut pattern sections apart.

4. Change darts to gathers or relocate where needed.

5. Add seam allowances.

To Sew: Make facings for Designs A and D band sections. Use interfacing for bands. Sew bands together on outside edge. Press and attach to rest of bodice. Make spaghetti straps for Design B. Use buttons, hooks, or allow additional fabric for tie for halter, Design C.

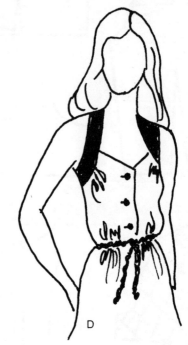

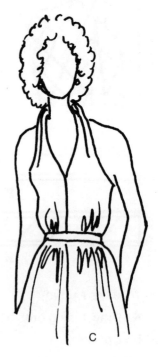

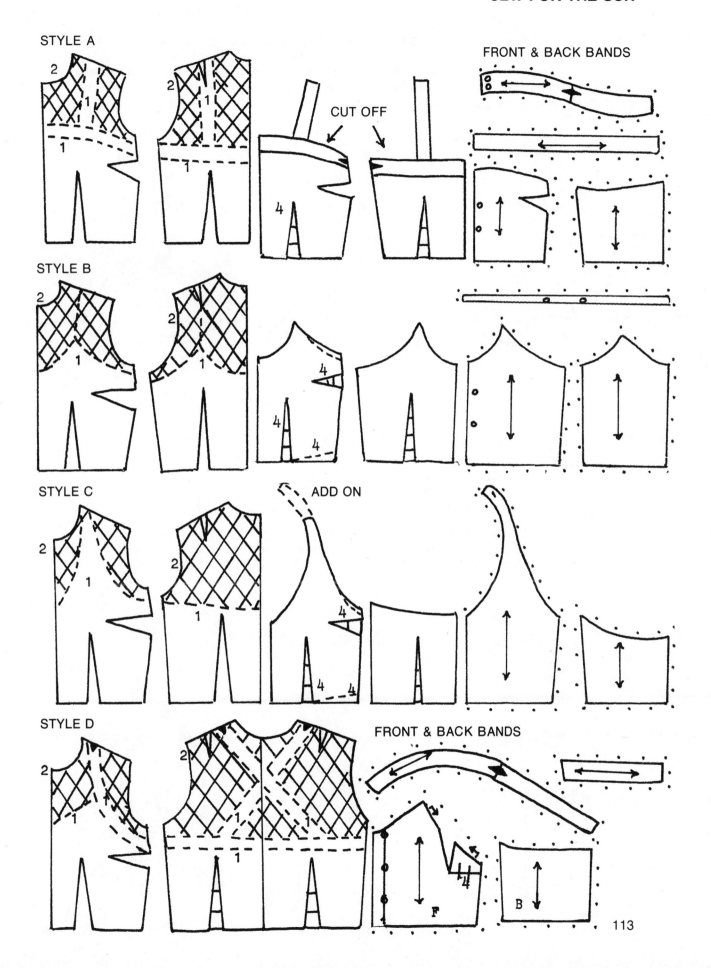

STYLE A

FRONT & BACK BANDS

CUT OFF

STYLE B

STYLE C

ADD ON

STYLE D

FRONT & BACK BANDS

FRECKLES AND PIGTAILS

Oh, the beautiful little dresses that make your precious one look like a doll. And you can make any design now, using the design cuts in these lessons to guide you. For years, I've collected pictures from magazines and newspapers and get many good ideas from them. Children's styles do not change as much as adults' but do incorporate some of the current trends. You can make a basic pattern for your child, using the method in this book. They are much easier than making an adult pattern since there is so little shaping. It shouldn't be any problem for you. Have fun!

THE MASCULINE GENDER

We mustn't forget about the men in our life. If you love tailoring clothes, you can really shine in this area. You can draft shirt patterns or you can take a ready-made that fits well, cut it out on the seamlines (you will add seams when cutting new shirt out), make any adjustments that you want, and you're ready to go. Pay close attention to the new trends in collars as these are what change most often. Commercial patterns use too-large collars as a rule, and this is a give-away of the home-made look. Be sure and take notice of collar size and shape.

Since man first learned to fit sleeves into a garment, the styles for sleeves have become varied and have run the gamut. Sleeves can be just a necessary item for a garment or they can be a dramatic focal point. An otherwise plain garment comes to life when a decorative sleeve is added. They can definitely be the determining factor of an attractive gown.

In the following chapter, we will study all of the basic sleeve styles and then some. But you can elaborate on these styles and change them to suit the current fashion.

Well-fitting sleeves that hang properly are so important to a garment. The way a sleeve fits a garment is determined upon how it is cut. The sleeve caps must match the armhole curves perfectly and there should be just enough ease. Too much ease can destroy the appearance or eye appeal. Notice below in the sketch how the caps of the sleeve match up with the armhole curves of the bodices.

To sew a sleeve properly, you must stay-stitch all the way around the cap. This allows the ease to be worked out evenly. Also, some fabrics just do not all ease the same and there is no way that you can work the ease out of the upper part of the sleeve. This gives you the advantage of being able to work it out at the bottom of the cap.

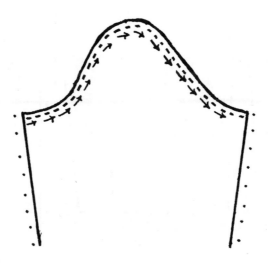

SLEEVE SESSION

STYLE #1 — THE SHIRT SLEEVE: This pattern is for a woman's shirt sleeve. A man's sleeve has less fullness at the bottom of the sleeve just above the cuff. They are usually tapered from the elbow down and will have one or two pleats to none at all.

Pattern Construction:

1. Determine cuff width. Cut this amount off of your basic sleeve pattern.

2. Lay sleeve pattern on a piece of paper. Tape down.

3. Draw straight lines from sleeve cap down, extending 1 inch below bottom edge. This is ease for sufficient movement.

4. Draw a line for sleeve bottom, curving slightly toward center. This gives extra room for elbow ease.

5. Mark sleeve placket. There are three ways to make a placket (see following page).

6. Mark sleeve bottom for gathers or pleats.

7. Make cuff pattern. Directions for making cuffs can be found on page 120 of this chapter.

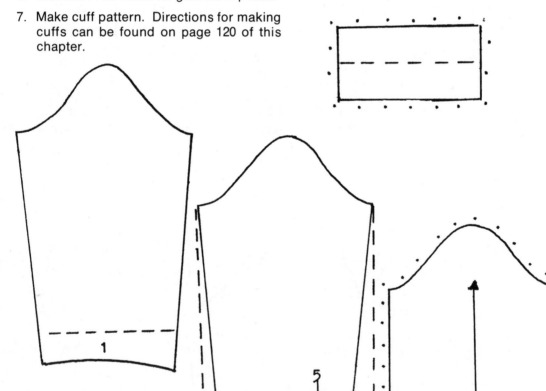

SLEEVE PLACKETS

Plackets generally are positioned 2 to 2-1/2 inches in from back side of sleeve. This is determined by the cuff. Divide the cuff measurement into quarters. Use 1/4 for the measurement between back side of sleeve and placket.

THREE METHODS FOR PLACKETS

Pleat: This is the easiest and neatest of the three methods but is not used on men's shirts. It is used on men's leisure jackets.

Binding: This is a traditional method.

Facing: This, too, is a traditional method and gives a finished look.

DIRECTIONS:

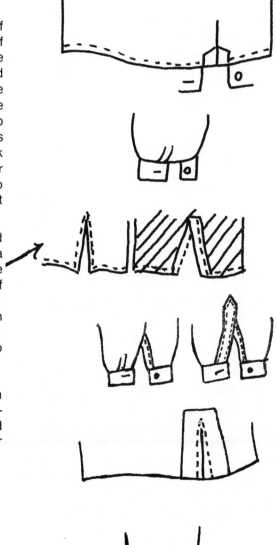

Pleat: Use 1/2 inch on either side of placket line for pleat. Sew cuff onto the sleeve bottom with the front of the cuff ending at one end of the pleat allowance and the back of the cuff ending at the other end of pleat allowance. Clip the pleat allowance at the ends and turn under and stitch. Tack 1/2 inch of this allowance under the front section of your cuff to form permanent pleat. Doesn't it look neat?

Binding: Slit placket 2-1/2 inches and stay-stitch. Clip point. Take a strip of fabric 1-1/2 inches wide and 6 inches long; sew one side of strip to the wrong side of placket. Fold over to right side and turn under 1/4 inch and top-stitch. Tailored placket may be added to front side of sleeve.

Facing: Cut a piece of fabric as diagram indicates. Sew to placket, forming a point at the top. This should be 2-1/2 inches. Clip in the center of the stitches. Turn and press.

117

SLEEVE SESSION

STYLE #2 — THE BISHOP SLEEVE: The bishop sleeve has been around for a long time and is very feminine. It can have just a few gathers or many gathers, a short or long cuff or even just a binding for a cuff. Remember, the fuller the sleeve, the dressier.

Pattern Construction:

1. Determine cuff width and cut off basic sleeve pattern.

2. Divide into six sections.

3. Cut through lines to within 1/4 inch of top of pattern.

4. Spread sections to desired amount of fullness.

5. Add 1 to 1-1/2 inch to the bottom to give a nice roll over the cuff.

   For short-sleeve version, cut off sleeve pattern and follow above steps.

STYLE #3 — THE PEASANT SLEEVE: This sleeve is different from the bishop sleeve in that it has fullness at the top of the sleeve also. The puffed sleeve is a short variation of this — see short versions on diagrams.

Pattern Construction:

1. Determine cuff width and cut off basic sleeve pattern.

2. Draw a line between caps.

3. Draw six lines across pattern.

4. Number both top and bottom sections. (You'll be sorry if you don't — you might misplace a section.)

5. Cut the sections apart. Cut the cross lines.

6. When you pull the upper sections apart, you will notice that you lose most of the curve. To restore some of this, move upper section upward. Of course, the fullness of your pattern will determine how much you will move the pieces.

7. Add 1 to 1-1/2 inches at the bottom of sleeve.

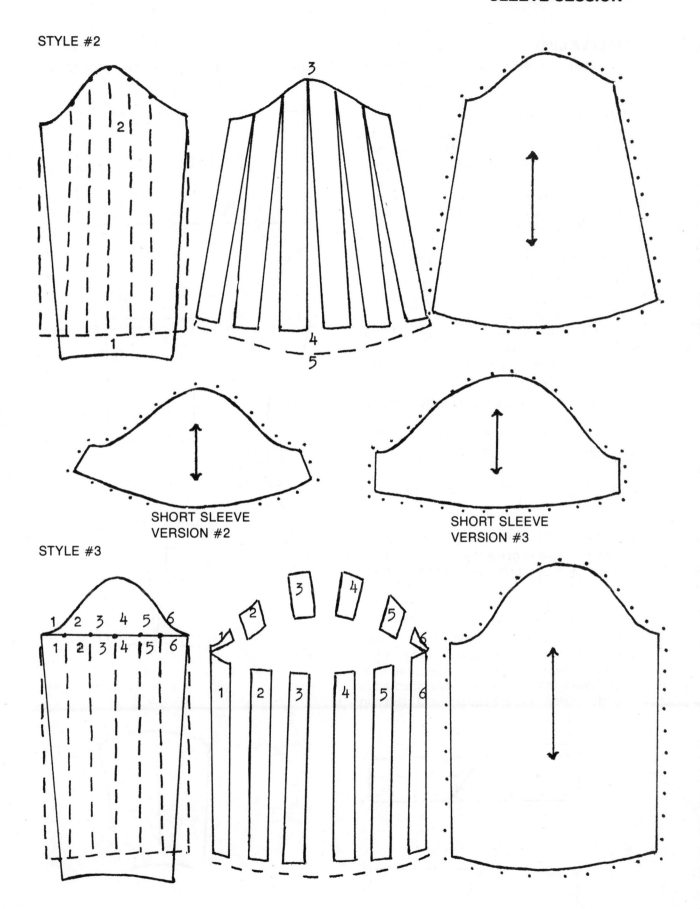

STYLE #2

3

2

1

4

5

SHORT SLEEVE
VERSION #2

SHORT SLEEVE
VERSION #3

STYLE #3

1 2 3 4 5 6
1 2 3 4 5 6

2 3 4 5

1   6

1   2   3   4   5   6

119

SLEEVE SESSION

SLEEVE CUFF

Cuffs are always in style but will go from very narrow to extremely wide from season to season.

The Straight Cuff:

Draw a cuff pattern on a piece of paper 2 inches longer than your wrist measurement and double the desired cuff width. This will allow for the button foldover. Add 3/8-inch seam. This cuff is folded and forms its own facing. It should have firm interfacing cut to fit finished cuff.

The Shaped Cuff: This cuff fits the arm snugly.

1. Determine cuff length.
2. Measure the wrist and the area at the point of the top of the cuff.
3. Cut a strip of paper the width of your wrist measurement (plus 1/2 inch for ease) and the desired length of cuff. This is for buttons with loops.
4. Cut this strip at the center from the top down, leaving 1/4 inch at bottom. Spread apart to the upper measurement plus 1/2 inch for ease.
5. Add 3/8-inch seam allowance.
6. You will use a facing and interfacing for cuff.

The Bias Cuff: Use this on a dressy-type dress.

The bias cuff is generally 1/2 inch wide so use a strip of fabric 1-3/4 inches wide and the length of your wrist plus 1-inch ease and 3/8 inches on either end for seam allowance. This is to be cut on bias.

NOTE: If fabric is not too heavy, double width on the fabric strip. You will fold this before sewing to sleeve. It gives a smoother appearance and also gives a finished edge underneath. This will allow you to "stitch in the ditch."

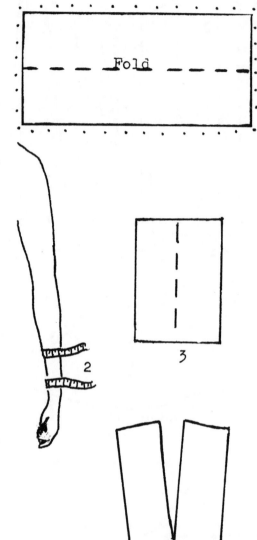

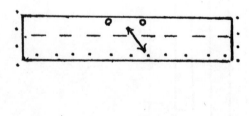

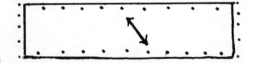

STYLE #4 — THE BISHOP SLEEVE WITH SHAPED CUFF: May be just what you need to set off that dress you're making!

Pattern Construction:

1. Determine cuff depth and draw the cuff design onto basic pattern. Cut off.

2. Measure your wrist and the portion of your arm where the cuff top will be. Add 1/2 to 1 inch for ease.

3. Apply above measurement to the cuff design on your pattern. Cut off excess.

4. **Draw five lines on upper pattern using point of design for center line.**

5. Cut through lines, leaving 1/4 inch at top. Spread to desired fullness.

NOTE: So that point on the cuff will be nice and sharp, sew away from the point on both sides.

SLEEVE SESSION

STYLE #5 — LEG O'MUTTON SLEEVE: I have no idea how this sleeve got its name, but it is pretty. It was used in designs back in the 1940's and will probably make a comeback soon. It is already appearing on wedding gowns.

Pattern Construction:

1. Draw a line at the elbow of basic sleeve pattern. Cut apart.

2. Draw three lines on upper portion.

3. Cut from top down to within 1/4 inch of bottom.

4. Spread to desired fullness.

5. Add additional height to curve.

6. Re-attach bottom portion.

To Sew: You may want to take out some of the fullness from the elbow down. If so, leave 2 inches un-sewn at the bottom of the sleeve to facilitate ease of pulling over the hand.

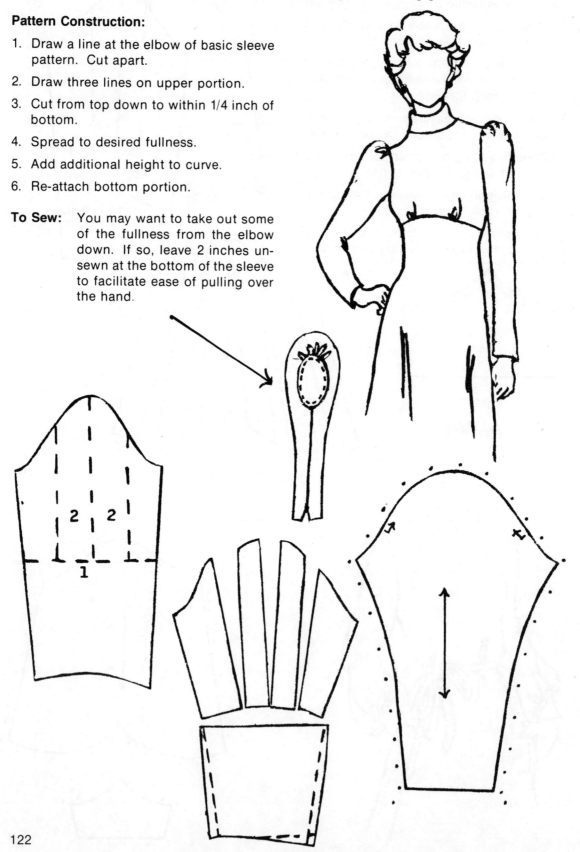

STYLE #6 — THE TULIP SLEEVE: I think when you look at this sleeve you will see why it is called by this name. I used this design on a dress for my daughter when she was five. The dress was white with tiny crochet trim. The only ornament was a 1/2-inch black velvet tie belt on which I attached small pink rosebuds to the ends.

Pattern Construction:

1. You will use two sleeve patterns for this design. Cut off both patterns at desired length.

2. Draw a curve on front portion of one of the patterns, 1 to 2 inches beyond the center.

3. Repeat with second pattern but draw curve to the back cap.

4. Cut excess from both patterns.

5. Make complete facing if sheer fabric is used. Otherwise, use 1-1/2-inch facing or piping to finish sleeve.

6. For gathered tulip, slice and spread.

To Sew: Sew front and back sections together at caps. Repeat for facing. Sew facing to sleeve. Match shoulders of sleeve so that they overlap. Stay-stitch. Sew into armhole.

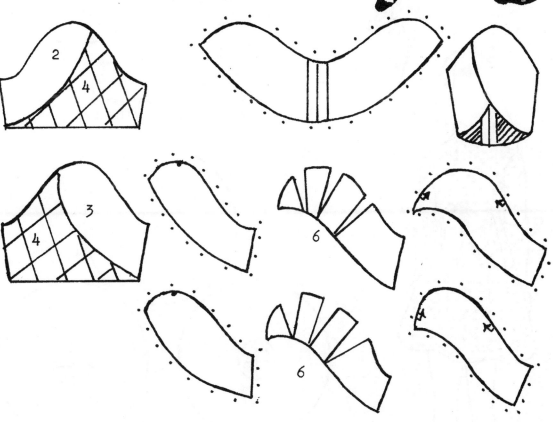

SLEEVE SESSION

STYLE #7 — SLEEVE WITH RIPPLED FLOUNCE: There are two kinds of flounces and each one gives a distinct look. The first is always lined and does not fall in cascades but has a soft, rippled effect. The second is very full and falls in cascades on the arm or wrist.

Pattern Construction:

Remember the ruffled collar that we constructed in the chapter on collars? The same principle exists here. You may either use a strip of paper the width of the measurement of the bottom part of the sleeve and the length you wish or you may use a dessert plate for your pattern. Follow directions for the ruffled collar. Have fun!

SLEEVE MEASUREMENT

FLOUNCE WIDTH

One CIRCLE FOR PATTERN #1
TWO CIRCLES FOR PATTERN #2

DESSERT PLATE

STYLE #8 — THE ANGEL SLEEVE: I don't know where this sleeve got its name. Maybe it's because, when used on a long sleeve, it would give the effect of wings when the arm was raised. Or, maybe it's because the dress is SO feminine.

Pattern Construction:

1. Determine length of sleeve. Cut off unnecessary portion. We will make a short version for demonstration.

2. Draw six lines on the pattern for a moderately full sleeve and up to ten lines for a very full sleeve.

3. Cut through lines from bottom to within 1/4 inch of top.

4. Spread to desired fullness.

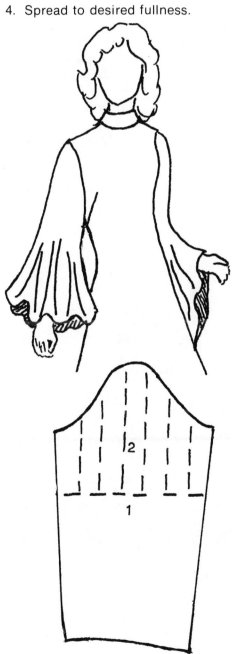

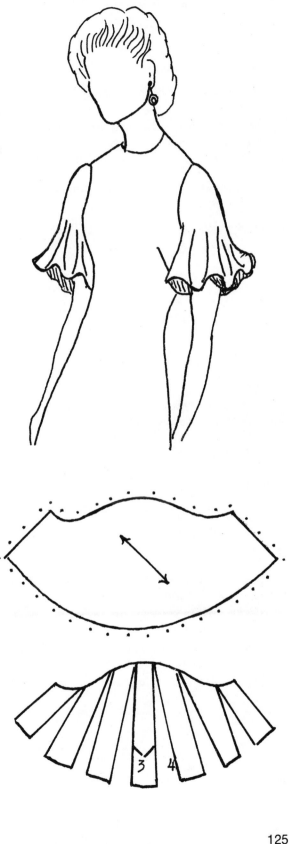

SLEEVE SESSION

STYLE #9 — THE BELL SLEEVE: I remember one time that I was introduced to a woman at a gathering. I don't remember the woman but I remember her dress. It was perfectly plain with the exception of the sleeves. The dress was made from a fabric that was a brown and white mixture, closely woven to give the effect of being tan. It had a round neck piped in brown and bell sleeves lined in burnt orange with brown piping at the edge. Very elegant!

Pattern Construction:

1. Cut off sleeve pattern at elbow. Discard bottom.

2. Draw a line between the caps. Draw five lines on the sleeve portion.

3. Cut across the horizontal line.

4. Cut to within 1/4 inch of the top on the sleeve portion.

5. Spread sections to desired fullness.

A

THE LONG BELL

I used this type of sleeve on one of my daughter's wedding gowns. The sleeves draped beautifully as she held her bouquet.

Pattern Construction:

1. Cut basic sleeve pattern at elbow. Draw five lines on bottom portion.

2. Cut to within 1/4 inch of top.

3. Spread to desired fullness.

4. Re-attach to top of sleeve.

NOTE: The long bell can be cut either on the straight of grain or on the bias.

B

STYLE #9 (A)

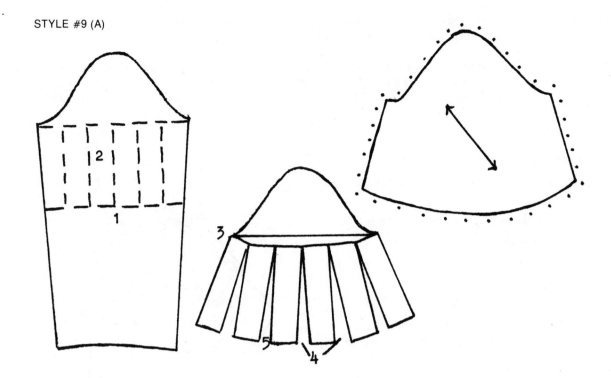

STYLE #9 (B)

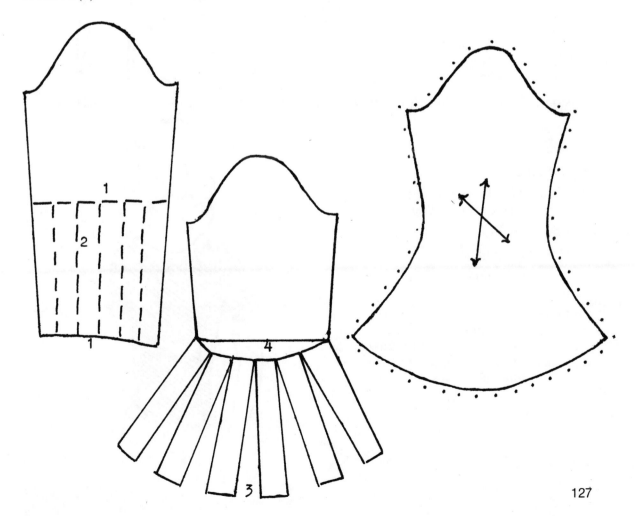

SLEEVE SESSION

STYLE #10 — THE DECORATIVE SLEEVE: This is a series of sleeves to show what can be done to add extra sleeve interest.

Version 1 – I used this one the first time I ran short of fabric for one of my daughter's dresses. Fortunately, it was the focal point of the dress and she got many compliments. I had enough scraps to cut the sleeve in separate pieces but not enough to cut the sleeve whole.

Pattern Construction:

1. Cut a sleeve pattern off at the desired length.

2. Draw line down center of sleeve.

3. Cut and spread apart.

4. Add extension at bottom of front side for buttons.

5. Make facing pattern.

To Sew: Sew the underarm seam together first. Sew underarm of **facing**. Attach to bottom of sleeve. Finish by sewing the portion of the sleeve from the extension up.

Version 2 – I have used this style both with and without underfacing. It adds that final touch.

Pattern Construction:

1. Cut off pattern at desired length.

2. Draw a line down the center of the pattern to get the right spot for design point.

3. Draw in design.

4. Make facing pattern.

5. Make an underfacing pattern if you plan to use one.

To Sew: Sew underarms together. Sew facing together. Pin to sleeve. Sew from the point outward on both sides from the point. See enlarged view on diagrams.

VERSION #1

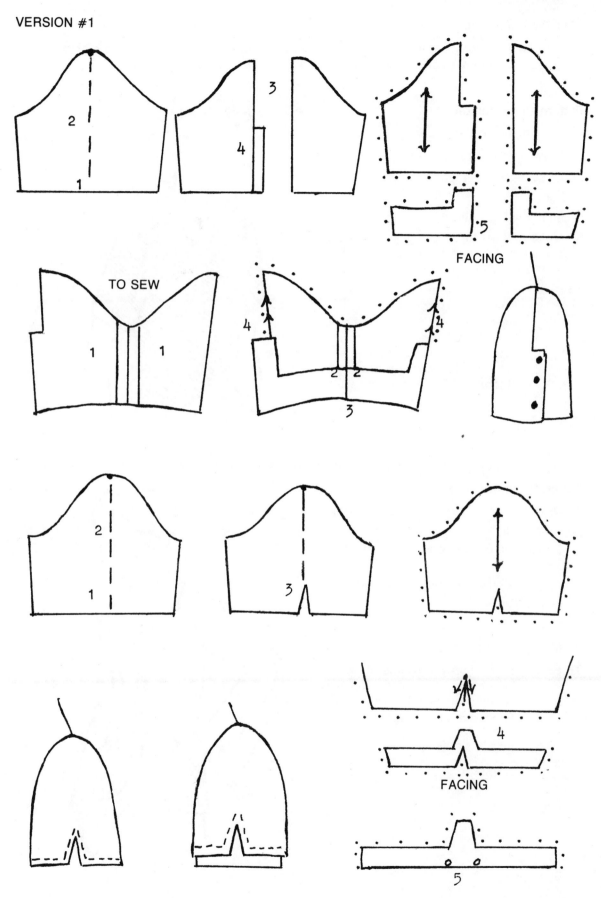

TO SEW

FACING

FACING

STYLE #10 (cont'd)

Version 3 – This design will give you a clever way to add that touch of white to a dress, but don't limit yourself to white. Try other color combinations too.

Pattern Construction:

1. Cut off sleeve pattern.

2. Draw line through center.

3. Draw design using line to center the design.

4. Make facing pattern.

5. Make pattern for inset by following design. Use 1/2 inch for extension and 1 inch for seams. Double for fold.

To Sew: Sew underarm seams of sleeve. Sew facing together, Pin to sleeve and sew. Turn and press. Sew underfacing together. Fold over and stitch together to secure. Attach to sleeve by top-stitching 1/2 inch onto sleeve.

Version 4 – This style is particularly pretty on a coat or jacket with a loose-fitting style. I also saw it done on a dress which was very stunning; the sleeves were three-quarter.

Pattern Construction:

1. Draw line down center of sleeve pattern. Cut apart.

2. Lay sleeve pattern on a piece of paper. Tape.

3. Add extension to sides and centers of sections.

4. Curve center line at bottom.

5. Make facing pattern.

To Sew: Sew underarm seams of sleeve. Sew facing. Sew to sleeve. Sew center seam last. Turn and press. Top-stitch (see Diagram A).

STYLE #10, Version 3

STYLE #10, Version 4

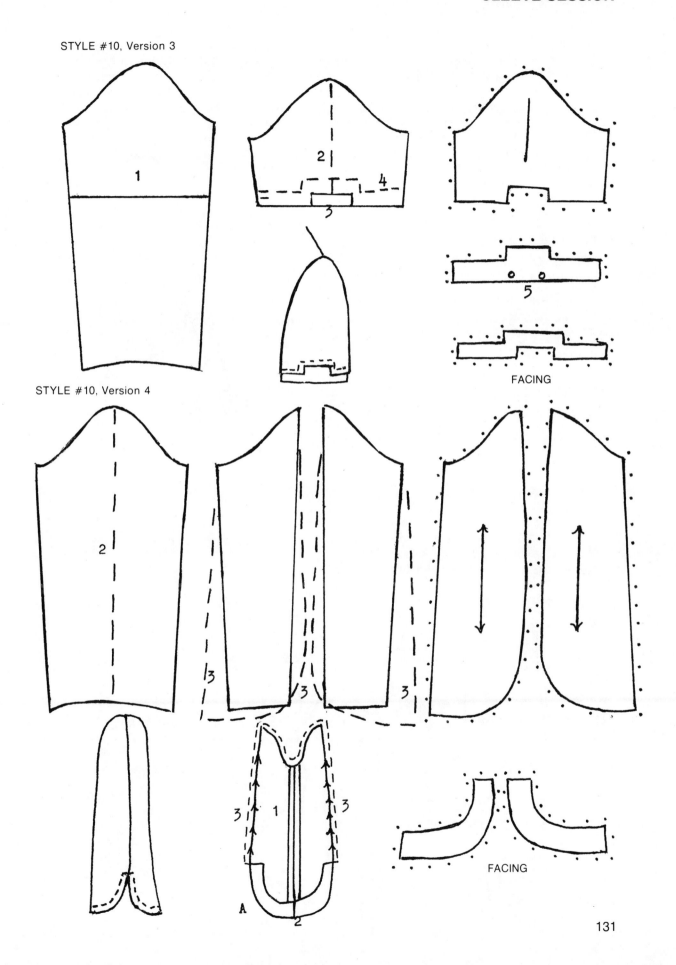

FACING

FACING

STYLE #11 — THE SHIRRED SLEEVE: When one of my daughters was to be married, I tried to decide upon the design of the dress that I was to wear. I found a large pin in my jewelry box (a series of varied type stones in seafoam green) that I had never worn because I had never had just the right dress. I found a soft fabric in a matching color and designed my dress around *that* pin. I used the pin at the waistline to pull a shirred midriff into a point at the center. To set the dress off even more, I used the shirred sleeve. It was elegant — I loved it! And it didn't look like a rack dress.

Pattern Construction:

1. Lay a large piece of paper under a basic sleeve pattern. Tape at the top of the sleeve but leave the bottom free.

2. Trim sides of sleeve to fit arm measurement with 1-inch ease.

3. Draw a line from your dart control to the bottom of the pattern.

4. Cut this line and pull the dart control together. Tape.

5. Draw six lines from the dart control to the bottom on the opposite side.

6. Number them (PLEASE)!

7. Cut the sections apart and spread to desired fullness, which depends upon the weight of the fabric.

To Sew: Sew two double rows of stitching on either side of front section and equal distances apart on center portion. Pull stitches so that front section fits the back section. Sew from dart control down, joining the two sections. Then sew the underarm seams, leaving 1-1/2 inches unsewn for snap.

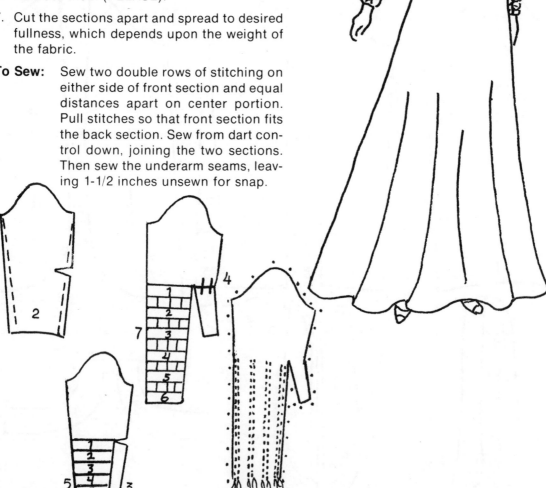

STYLE #12 — THE PLEATED TOP SLEEVE: This is a pretty sleeve that comes and goes in the fashion world.

Pattern Construction:

1. Draw a line on your sleeve pattern from cap to cap.

2. Determine where you want your pleats and draw onto pattern. Draw lines through to center of bottom.

3. Cut horizontal line and then the slanted lines.

4. Spread apart to desired fullness for pleats (usually an inch).

5. Tape to bottom of sleeve.

6. For tuck at bottom of sleeve, add 1 inch to each side.

To Sew: Fold pleat either toward or away from center of cap. Stay-stitch. Sew into garment as you normally would.

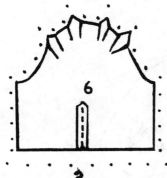

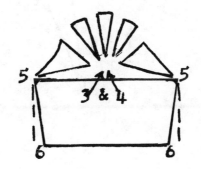

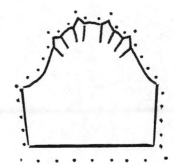

SLEEVE SESSION

STYLE #13 — THE KIMONO SLEEVE: The Kimono sleeve gets its origin from the Japanese Kimono. The original Kimono was a very basic design. A large rectangle formed the body and a small rectangle formed the sleeve. The style has gone through many changes and has been modified. Below are several versions. You will find that this sleeve is very comfortable and has always been popular in one form or another.

Version 1 – This is a modified but still loose-fitting version.

Pattern Construction:

1. Take a bodice pattern front and a bodice pattern back and tape shoulder seams at neck. Leave 1/2 inch open at armholes.

2. Fold down cap of sleeve pattern.

3. Attach to bodices as diagram indicates.

4. Draw line from neck to bottom of sleeve.

5. Cut apart.

6. Underarm seam may be curved to obtain desired amount of fullness.

7. Eliminate side dart.*

To Sew: Sew shoulder-arm seams. Sew underarm seams. Reinforce with tape on the stress area under the arm.

* If there is too much ease to work into the side seam in order to fit the back seam, you may take the needed amount off at waistline.

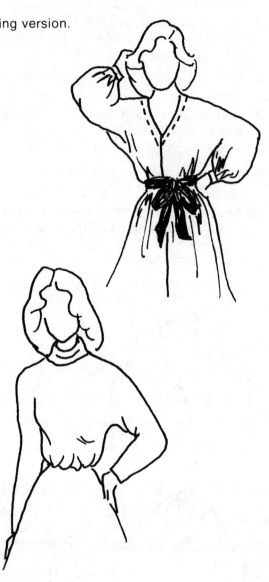

STYLE #13 — KIMONO

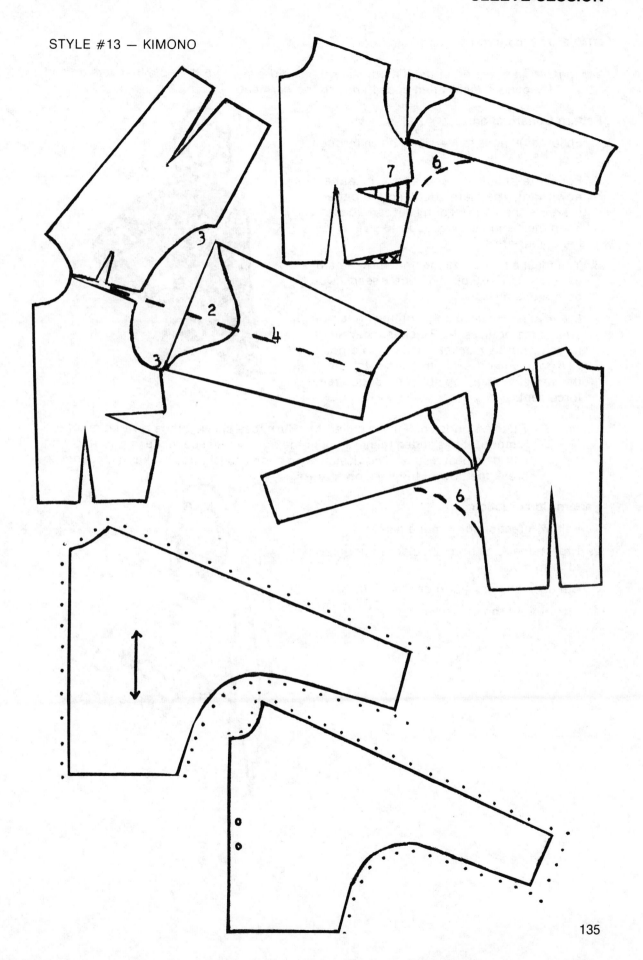

STYLE #13 (cont'd)

Version 2 – This version of the Kimono sleeve has more shaping than the first version and gives a more fitted appearance to the garment.

Pattern Construction:

1. Follow directions for Version 1 down through Step #5.

2. For more shaping, bend sleeve of pattern downward. The more you bend the pattern, the more shaping, but don't get carried away. Keep the design easy enough to give as you bend your arms.

3. You must either curve the underarm area or use gussets. Use tape to reinforce seam if you do not use gussets.

4. *For gussets:* Slice an angle on the underarm area of the bodices 2-1/2 inches. Stay-stitch as you would a placket, stitching to a point. Clip point. Pin gusset to this and stitch along the stay-stitching. Top-stitch for added reinforcement.

Version 3 – This version is sometimes called the Burnoose sleeve but is a variation of the Kimono. It has added fullness under the arm. It must be made in a soft-flowing fabric for best results. This design is great on a tall figure as it has a tendency to break the flow of the lines on a dress.

Pattern Construction:

1. Follow direction for Kimono sleeve.

2. Draw three lines from shoulder to underarm to form rays.

3. Cut lines and spread to desired fullness.

4. Smooth out top of sleeve.

STYLE #13. Version 2

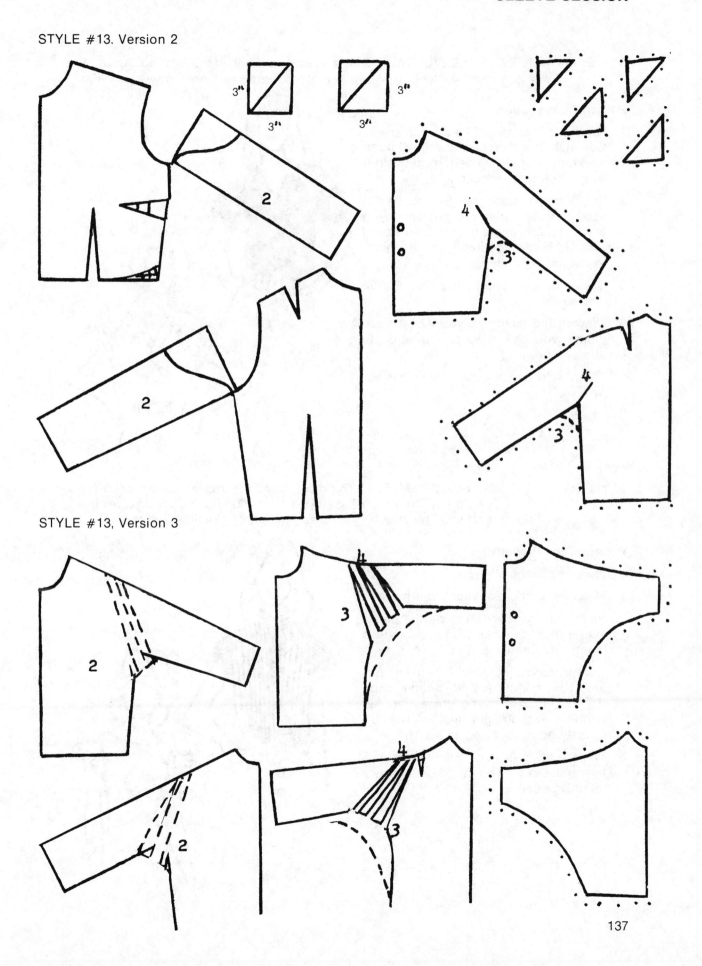

STYLE #13, Version 3

STYLE #14 — THE CAP SLEEVE: This sleeve is a short variation of the Kimono sleeve. For a cool summer dress, it is a winner. It also works well on jumpers for winter.

Pattern Construction:

1. For the longer version of the cap sleeve (see A), follow directions for the Kimono sleeve but cut sleeve pattern to desired length before constructing.

2. For shorter version (see B), you do not need to use your sleeve pattern. Lay a piece of paper under the armhole area. (I make my drawing directly on the fabric to cut down on steps.)

3. Draw addition onto the paper. Curve downward.

4. Draw in the facing. If you wish to use piping, you can make facing separate and sew on.

5. Fill in side dart if desired and cut out pattern.

STYLE #15 — THE SEWN-IN CAP SLEEVE: This gives the effect of a small sleeve or cuff and can be very pretty if you are using stripes or checks. Sleeve can also be cut on bias for effect. The circular cap is so feminine — try all variations.

Pattern Construction:

1. Lay out a piece of paper.

2. Measure armhole of your pattern.

3. Place your tape measure on the paper with it in a standing position. Curve to length of armhole. Dot in curve.

4. Draw in curve. (A) Connect with straight line. Use as fold line to double cap. (B) Add 1 inch to ends of curve and then connect with straight line to give cuff effect. Can be doubled as in (A).

5. This variation is made from sleeve pattern and is curved on the edge. It gives a fitted-type cap.

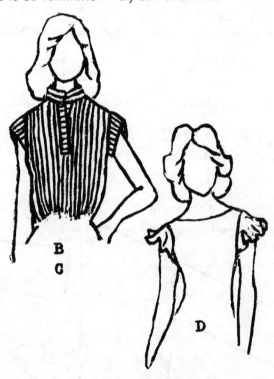

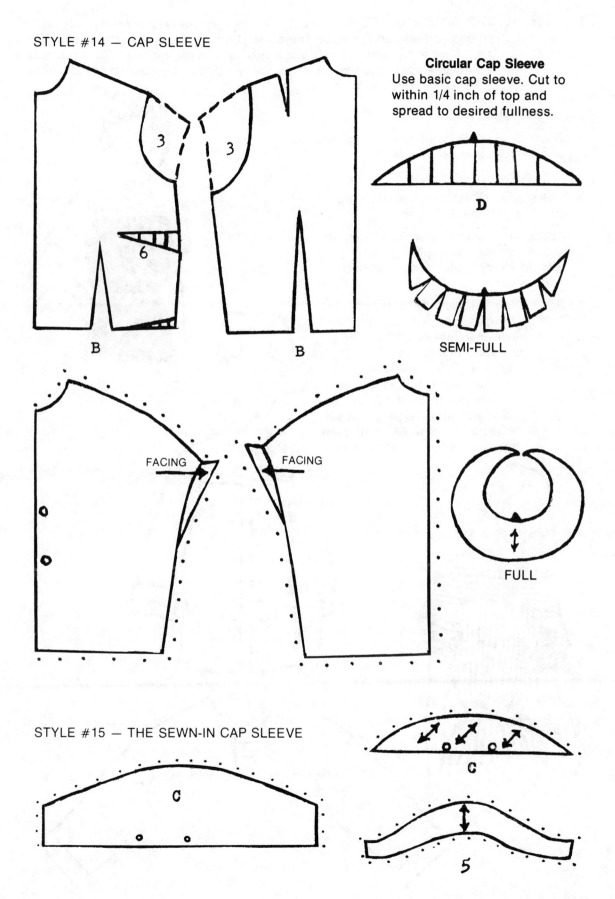

STYLE #14 — CAP SLEEVE

Circular Cap Sleeve
Use basic cap sleeve. Cut to within 1/4 inch of top and spread to desired fullness.

D

SEMI-FULL

B   B

FACING   FACING

FULL

STYLE #15 — THE SEWN-IN CAP SLEEVE

C

C

5

STYLE #15 — THE YOKE AND SLEEVE COMBO: This design is very lovely and is adaptable to both dresses and jackets. There are short and long sleeve versions. You might like to try combining two colors of fabrics for this one. You could also use bias stripes or checks for the yoke. But all one color is great — just top-stitch to accentuate the design.

Pattern Construction:

1. Draw design as diagram shows on bodice front and back patterns.

2. Cut apart.

3. Cut sleeve pattern to desired length. Draw center line. Cut apart.

4. Attach sleeve pattern to yoke as diagram shows. Be sure to slope the sleeve pattern downward. Close shoulder dart.

To Sew: You will ease the sleeve of this design as you normally do. If you use an opening for buttons on the yoke, finish at this time. Then clip the sleeve points and reinforce by stay-stitching. Pin yoke to bodice and sew the seam outward on either side of sleeve point. Sew shoulders and then the underarm and side seams.

STYLE #15

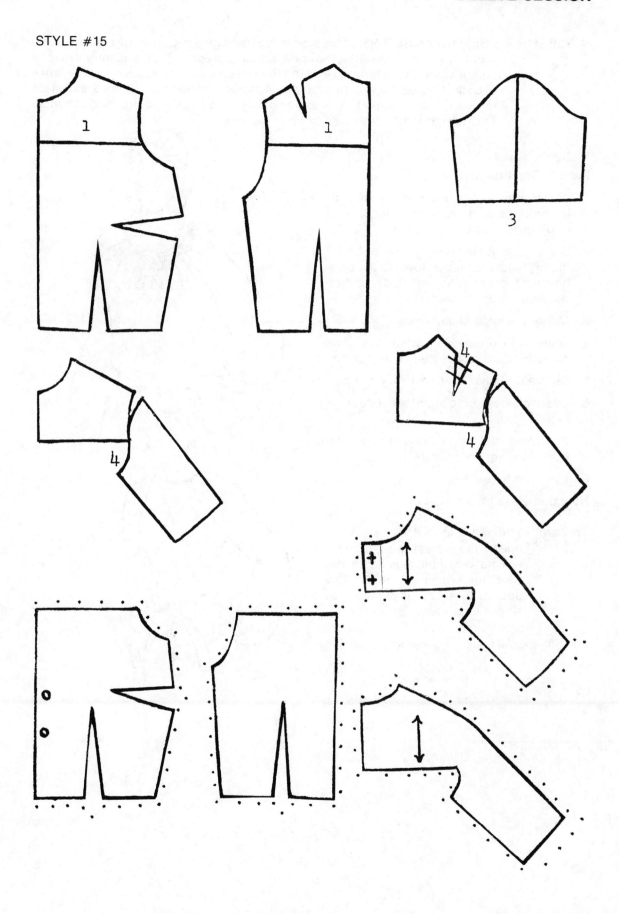

SLEEVE SESSION

STYLE #16 — THE RAGLAN SLEEVE: This sleeve has its origins in the Kimono sleeve but is more fitted than even the shaped Kimono sleeve. It is, you might say, a combination of the Kimono and the fitted sleeve as it includes characteristics of both. It gives the wearer freedom of movement and is, therefore, excellent to use in sports clothes. It also has beauty and is used in dressy garments. This design lends itself well to most fabrics.

Version 1

Pattern Construction:

1. Lower armholes on back and front bodice patterns by drawing off 3/4 inches at underarm. Cut away.

2. Draw a straight or curved line about 1-1/2 inches below shoulder down to the armhole curve on front and back bodice patterns. Mark shoulders.

3. Cut out — tape shoulders.

4. Draw lines on sleeve pattern that look something like a handle-bar mustache.

5. Cut sleeve lines to within 1/4 inch of top.

6. Overlap sleeve onto shoulder sections 1 inch. Tape.

7. Pull mustache up to the shoulder sections as diagram indicates.

8. Even armhole lines.

Now that wasn't hard, was it?

To Sew: You will find that this sleeve is one of the easiest to sew. There will be very little easing to do. Sew side seams of bodice. Sew underarm seam of sleeve. Pin sleeve to armhole. Sew in.

For Gathered Raglan: Follow steps on diagram.

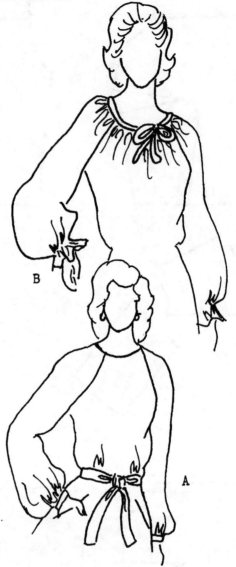

142

STYLE #16, RAGLAN SLEEVE

SCOOPED GATHERED RAGLAN

FOLLOW SLEEVE STEPS ABOVE
BUT CUT AND SPREAD FOR GATHERS

STYLE #16 (cont'd)

Version 2 – This version of the Raglan sleeve has a shoulder dart. If you have ever made a dress with this type sleeve, you know how difficult it is to get the shoulder dart to look right. Some patterns run the dart down onto the arm; it does not look good. To look good, the dart should cease at the end of the shoulder line. Try this design and see if you don't agree. This Raglan sleeve can be worked into firmer fabrics to give more fit while Version 1 does best with knits that stretch.

Pattern Construction:

1. Lower armholes on back and front bodice patterns by drawing off 3/4 inch at underarm. Cut away.

2. Draw a straight or curved line about 1-1/2 inches below shoulder down to the armhole curve on front and back bodice patterns. Mark shoulders.

3. Cut out — tape shoulders only at the armhole. Leave neck side open 1 to 1-1/2 inches for dart.

4. Follow remaining steps as in Version 1.

To Sew: Follow directions in Version 1.

STYLE #16 — RAGLAN SLEEVE

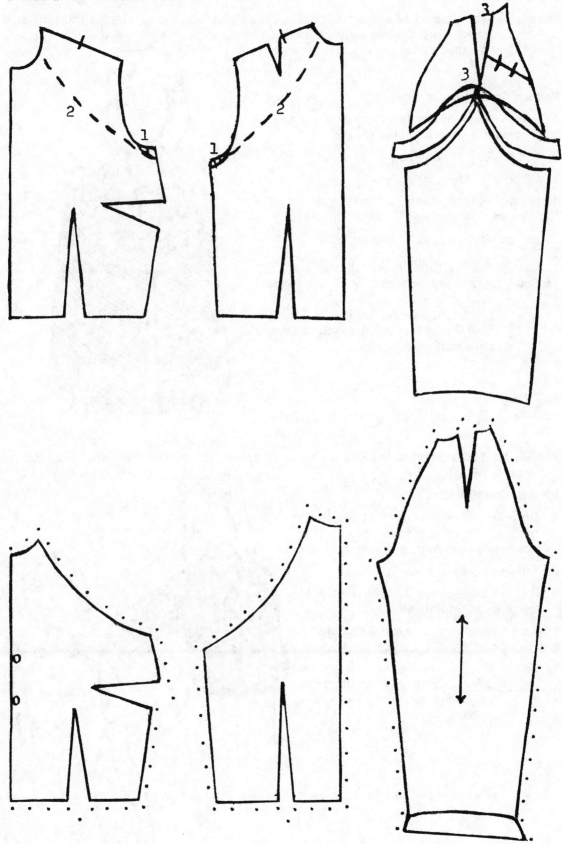

STYLE #16 (cont'd)

Version 3 – This version is used mostly on suit jackets, coats and housecoats, although I have seen it used effectively on tailored dresses. It gives a distinctive custom-designed look on any of the above.

Pattern Construction:

1. Draw lines on bodice front and back patterns as diagram shows. Label "F" and "B."

2. Cut yokes from bodices.

3. Close shoulder dart.

4. Divide sleeve pattern. Attach each half to front and back yokes. Tilt sleeve at an angle.

5. Smooth out lines on sleeve caps.

6. Add extension for fullness on sleeves.

To Sew: Sew A sections together. Press seam toward one side and top-stitch if desired. Sew B sections together. Press. Sew C sections together. Sew sleeves onto bodice.

Version 4 – This version of the Raglan is known as a strap shoulder. It gives variety to the design.

Pattern Construction:

1. Draw lines on bodice front and back parallel to the shoulder and 1 to 2 inches from shoulder. Mark shoulders.

2. Cut out yokes and tape together.

3. Attach sleeve pattern to shoulders, overlapping for smoothness.

That's it! The sleeve cap is not changed in this design.

To Sew: Ease sleeve as you naturally would. Sew from A in both directions after pinning sleeve onto bodice.

STYLE #16, Version 3

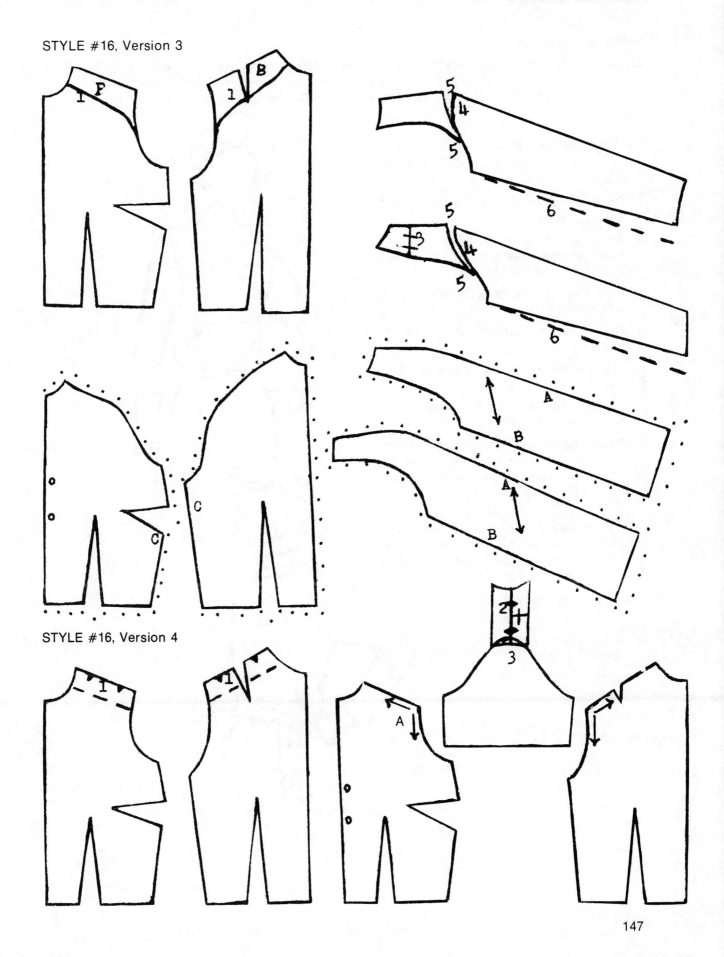

STYLE #16, Version 4

STYLE #16 (cont'd)

Version 5 – THE DOLMAN SLEEVE: This design can be considered as a variation of the Raglan sleeve but has the ease of the Kimono sleeve. It is used on suits, coats and dresses. This design makes a plain dress elegant.

Pattern Construction:

1. Determine design you will use. We'll use the square angle for demonstration.

2. Draw design on both bodice front and back patterns.

3. Attach bodice patterns at the neckline. Leave armhole side open 1/2 inch. Insert a piece of paper into the opening. Tape.

4. Fold back sleeve pattern cap. Attach sleeve pattern to bodices. Tape.

5. Cut out design. Disconnect bodices at neckline.

6. If you wish, the sleeve can be divided. See diagram.

7. You may use shoulder dart as is or you may change it to the sleeve seam.

To Sew: Sew shoulder seams of bodices. Lay open. Pin in sleeve. Sew in. Sew underarm of sleeve and bodice sides all in one.

For split sleeve – Sew each half of sleeve onto bodice front and back. Sew from neckline down to bottom of sleeve. Sew underarm and sides of bodice.

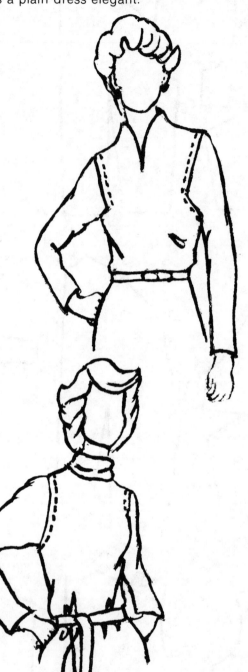

STYLE #16 — THE DOLMAN SLEEVE

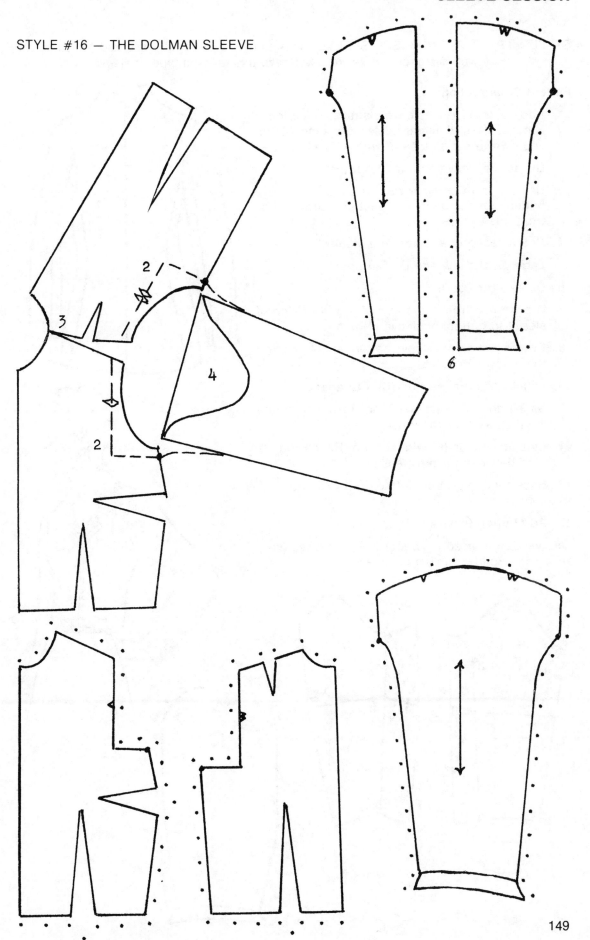

SLEEVE SESSION

STYLE #17 — THE TWO-PIECE SLEEVE: This sleeve is generally reserved for suits. All well-designed suit jackets will have this tailored type of sleeve.

Pattern Construction:

1. Add to bottom of sleeve pattern to increase width to desired fullness. Measure a jacket that you own to get an idea of what you want.

2. Divide the sleeve bottom into fourths.

3. Use the last quarter toward the back of sleeve pattern for the underarm section. Draw a line from this to cap.

4. Notch sections as diagram indicates.

5. Label Sections A and B. Cut apart.

6. Close elbow dart.

7. Draw a line from the curve of the front side of sleeve to bottom of sleeve. Notch.

8. Draw a line across sleeve pattern at the position the elbow would be.

9. Label underarm section (C). Cut apart.

10. Slice underarm section (C) on line and separate 1/2 inch as diagram shows.

11. Line up section (C) with section (B), leaving 1/2 inch between them for ease.

12. Slice section (A) from left to right. Separate 1/2 inch.

13. Add button extension if desired.

This version is used for decorative purposes (very effective). Follow numbers.

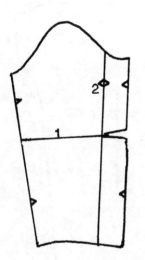
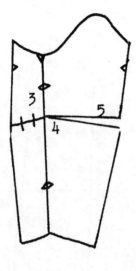

STYLE #17 — THE TWO-PIECE SLEEVE

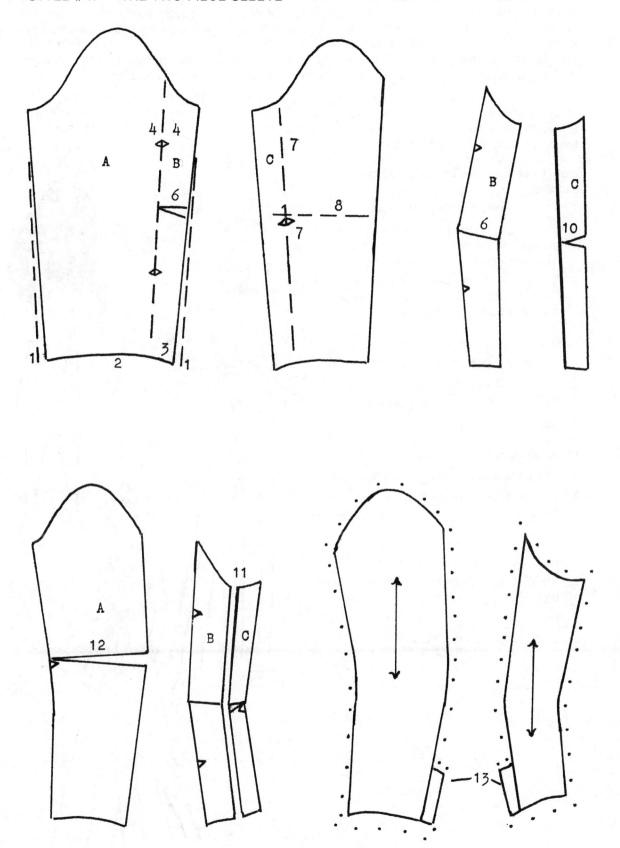

PANT PERFECTION

Amelia Bloomer was a leader in the movement for women's rights. She also created and wore the first pants for women in the United States. The baggy pants like those she originated still bear the *name bloomers*. Some women began wearing beach pajamas or knickers for active wear, but it wasn't until World War II that pants or slacks finally caught on. Women began wearing them to their jobs at defense plants because of their comfort. Slacks then progressed into all of society and are today one of the favorite fashions of women.

Styles in slacks change from year to year. They seem to rotate from flare to tight leg. But once you get a good stride fit, you may vary the style. A basic slack pattern can be used for any style slack, shorts, or skirt pants. I hope you will draft your own basic pant pattern from the directions in the last chapter.

How to change straight leg slacks to flare:

1. Place paper under legs of pant pattern. Tape.
2. For slight flare, place yardstick 2 inches above knee and swing yardstick outward to desired amount. Repeat for inside leg.
3. For more fitted flare, start about 3 inches below stride. Curve toward knee. Swing outward 2 inches above knee.

How to make a culotte skirt:

1. Cut pant pattern off at desired length.
2. A-line side of pattern.
3. Draw straight line on inside leg.
4. Make pleat if you wish.

How to make a circular pant skirt:

1. Cut pant pattern off at desired length.
2. Follow directions for A-line.
3. Draw line from dart control to bottom of skirt. Cut, spread.

How to make jump suit:

1. Attach bodice front to pant front pattern and tape.
2. Repeat for back.
3. Style of bodice can vary.

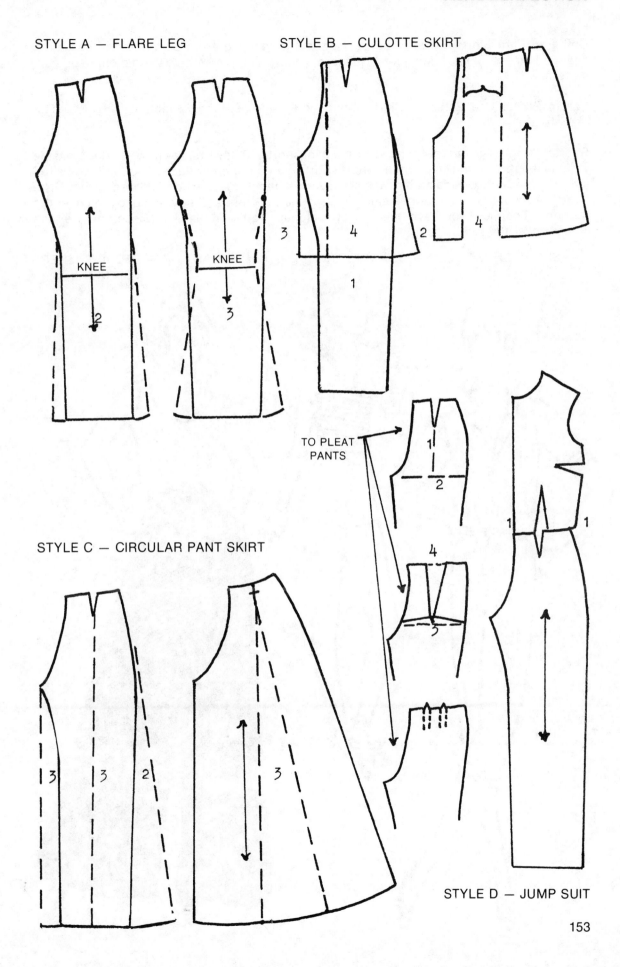

STYLE A — FLARE LEG

STYLE B — CULOTTE SKIRT

KNEE

KNEE

TO PLEAT
PANTS

STYLE C — CIRCULAR PANT SKIRT

STYLE D — JUMP SUIT

PANT PERFECTION

Gathered Pant Skirt: Divide basic pant pattern at dart control. Separate and spread to desired fullness. If you want a lot of fullness, you'll want to eliminate the hip curve on your pattern.

Harem Pants: Use Gathered Skirt pattern and use elastic at the ankle area instead of hemming.

Shorts: Your basic pant pattern can be used for shorts. Below you see a sketch denoting the various lengths. For all except the short shorts, you cut the pant pattern off at the desired length. Be sure to extend pattern at inside seam of hemline so the hem will turn up well. The short shorts are cut at an angle which is curved up in front and down in back to cover the derriere. The more you have, the more you curve. You'll be pleased to see how well the shorts cover the seat.

1 — SHORT SHORTS   2 — CITY SHORTS   3 — BERMUDAS   4 — PEDAL PUSHERS OR KNICKERS

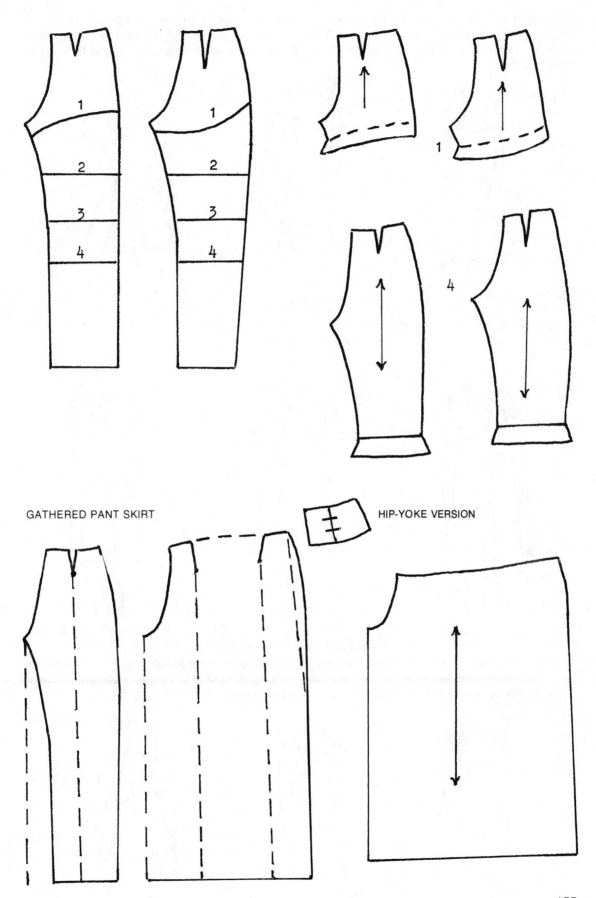

GATHERED PANT SKIRT

HIP-YOKE VERSION

TENNIS ANYONE?

For those of you who play tennis, you'll want to try your hand at creating a wardrobe of these. They are really just an extension of the pattern designs that we've already covered. You can even use your pant pattern, cut off, sliced and spread to accommodate fullness for the bloomers.

TEE OFF

Golf designs are also an extension of the pattern designs that we've already covered. Just get busy and see what lovelies you can make.

SLEEPING BEAUTY

Beautiful gowns are a must for every loving wife and they are SO expensive. I made each of my daughters a lingerie set for her trousseau. It's really a lot of fun to do. Here again, we go back to the previous pattern designs. See what you can do? And have fun!

 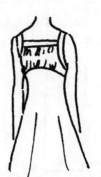 

156

THE ONE-PIECE CONSTRUCTION

One-piece dress designs come and go as all the other designs do. They have a prominent place in the designer's format for a number of years and then they disappear for a time, only to return with a flourish. The one-piece dress, as the name implies, may not be just one piece. It may have seams on the hipline or under the bust. Mainly, they are dresses that do not have waistline seams.

To make a one-piece pattern from your basic, you will need a flat, level edge. A dining table with a straight edge, a cutting board, a cabinet top, or even just a yardstick with a smooth edge will do.

Lay your basic bodice front and basic skirt front on the straight edge of whatever you are using. Slide together so that sides touch. Centers may or may not touch, depending upon your figure contour. Tape together; repeat for back.

You will note that there is an extension at the side of the bodice that extends beyond the skirt front. And you will note that most likely your skirt back extends beyond your bodice back. We take care of this, depending upon which style you will be working with, in the directions on the following pages.

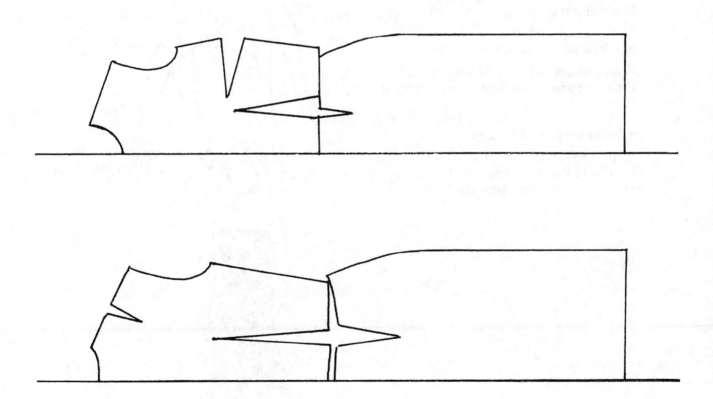

WAISTLESS WONDERS

STYLE #1 — THE STRAIGHT SHEATH: This design is for the trim figure. For the fuller figure, use less dart control or eliminate dart control altogether.

Pattern Construction:

1. Follow directions for constructing a one-piece dress pattern.

2. Lay a piece of paper under waist darts. Tape down.

3. Determine amount of fit you desire. This can be anywhere from skin-tight to an easy-fit. Use all of your dart control for a tight fit, less for an easy fit. We will use an inch for demonstration.

4. Draw a straight line through center of dart control. The bodice darts determine location of dart centers.

5. Fill in new dart control using an inch at the waistline.

6. Cut out new dart for ease in marking fabric.

7. Even out sides.

For Sheath with an A-Line Skirt:

Follow directions for a straight sheath with the exception of the skirt. Follow diagram to complete skirt.

For Chemise-Type Sheath:

Follow directions for straight sheath but eliminate darts at the waistline. Some chemise styles also eliminate the bust dart.

STYLE #1

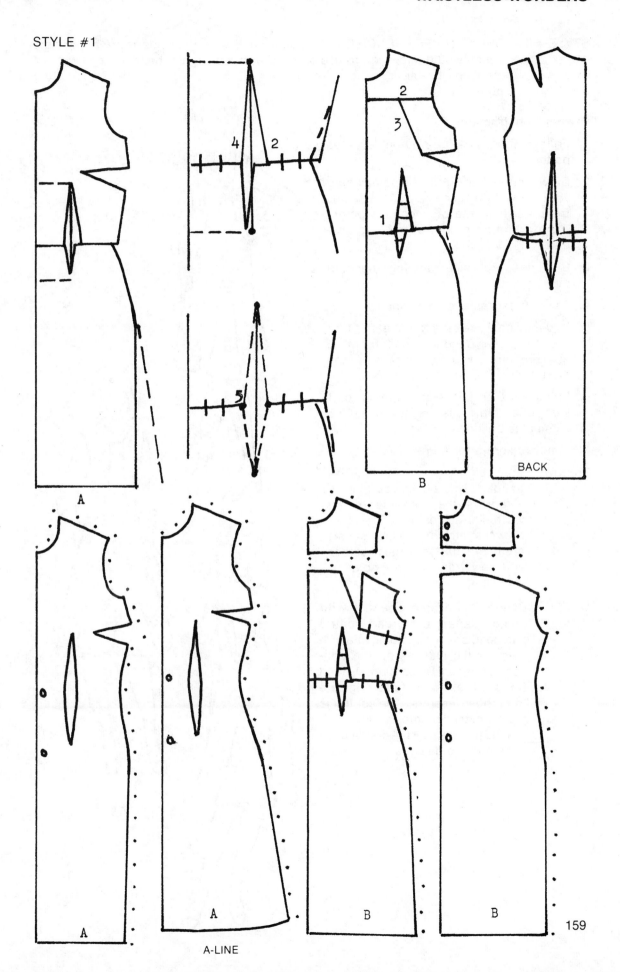

A-LINE

159

WAISTLESS WONDERS

STYLE #2 — SHEATH WITH FRENCH DART: You'll like this one. The darts are to the side, which would allow you to use a fabric with a design. The side darts will not interrupt the fabric design. The French darts are also very flattering to the figure.

Pattern Construction:

1. Follow directions for one-piece dress pattern.

2. Draw a curved line from the point where your hip widens (generally 3 to 4 inches from waist) to the bust control point. Draw a line from control point to side dart.

3. Cut lines. Pull side dart together and tape.

4. Take off excess at side of bodice.

5. You may now use as is for an easy fit, or you may make your dart deeper for more fit. *Remember,* you cannot take off any more than your skirt dart allows.

6. Use seam allowances around your dart legs to facilitate ease in sewing. Also eliminates bulkiness.

7. Follow diagram for A-line skirt.

To Sew: Stay-stitch along seam line on the dart. This allows you to ease in fabric so that both sides of dart will be the same. Sometimes fabric will stretch due to bias of dart area. Pin dart seams together and sew from control point to side seam.

NOTE: B and C are also sheaths with French darts but the dart control has been changed into seams. Remember the lessons on the princess styles in Discerning Divided Darts? These two styles originate from those lessons. The control is merely extended into the skirt. Follow the numbers on the diagrams to construct the designs.

160

STYLE #2

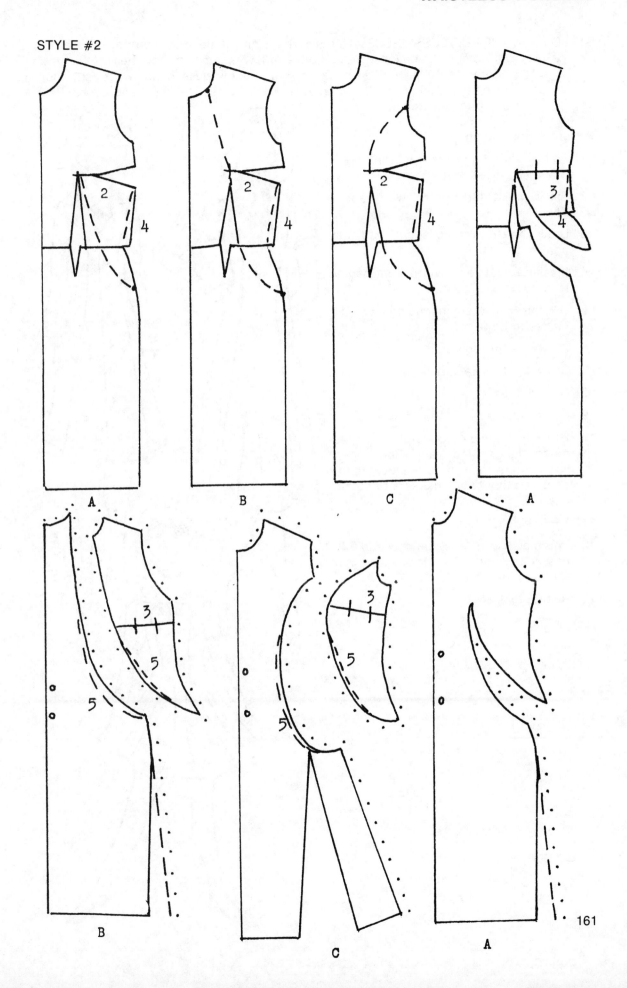

WAISTLESS WONDERS

STYLE #3 — THE PRINCESS DRESS: This is perhaps one of the most flattering designs for all women. It enhances a slim figure and will seem to take inches off the fuller figure. A woman with a full figure who took my class in pattern construction made this design up after we studied this in class. Her husband asked her if she had lost weight!

Pattern Construction:

1. Follow directions for constructing a one-piece dress pattern.

2. Fill in waist dart control with paper. Tape.

3. Draw a line from center shoulder to bust control point.

4. Measure waist dart width from center front to control point.

5. Use this measurement and dot every 12 inches to bottom of skirt.

6. Draw line through dots.

7. Draw line to side dart.

8. Cut on lines.

9. Close side dart.

10. Draw in new dart control, using as much ease as you want. Remember, you can only use amount allocated for control, but you can use less to obtain ease.

11. Fill in side of skirt.

12. You may use as is or you may add fullness to the skirt. Refer to six-gore skirt for directions.

13. Repeat for back.

STYLE #3

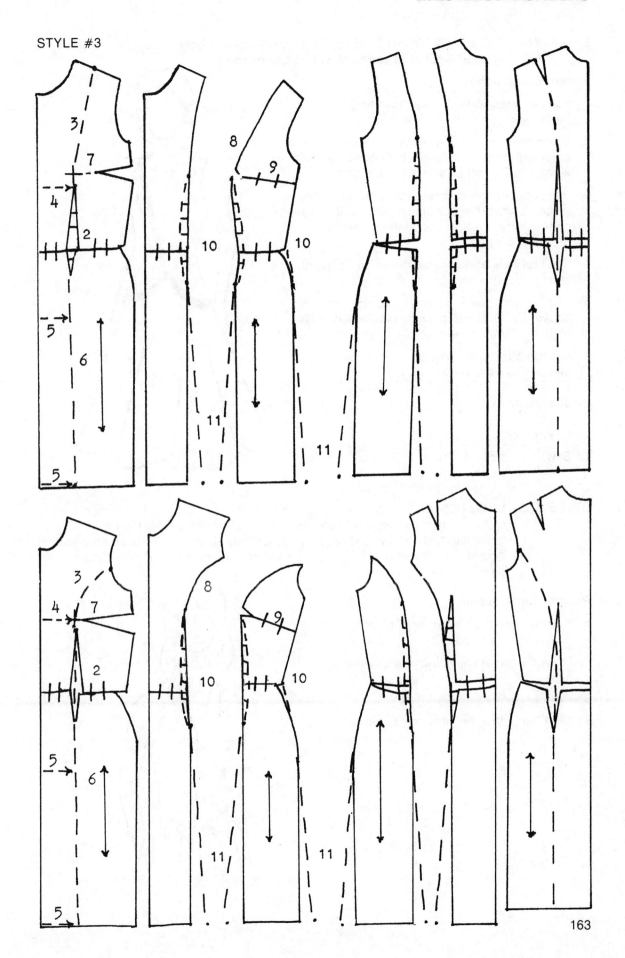

WAISTLESS WONDERS

STYLE #4 — THE LONG-TORSO DRESS: This design hasn't been around for a while, so you can expect to see a revival of it very soon.

Pattern Construction:

1. Follow directions for constructing a one-piece dress pattern.

2. Find point on your hip that you consider the most flattering, generally 6 to 8 inches below waistline. Cut off pattern at this point.

3. Use top portion in any of the various one-piece designs. For our diagram, we will use a chemise top with an asymmetric neckline. Striking, isn't it?

4. The first view of diagrams shows dart control changed to French dart.

5. The second view shows diagram for #3 above. Dart control may be eliminated. See page on Eliminating Darts.

6. Bottom portion of torso dress may be used in one of the ways listed below:
   a. A-line
   b. pleated
   c. gathered
   d. circular

To Sew: Complete the top portion of the dress, then attach skirt.

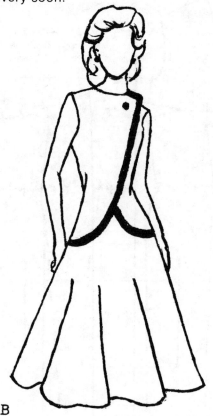

B

STYLE #5 — LOWERED WAISTLINE: Although this design is not truly a one-piece, the top or bodice of the dress has to be connected to the skirt before the design can be completed. This style never really goes out. It is always used in wedding gowns and lingerie, and it has a tendency to make your waistline appear smaller.

Pattern Construction:

1. Follow directions for constructing a one-piece dress pattern.

2. Draw design at waist, curving down into skirt.

3. Cut out.

4. Skirt can either be gathered or circular.

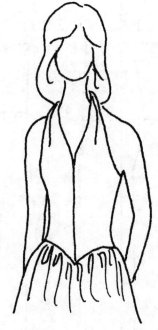

STYLE #4

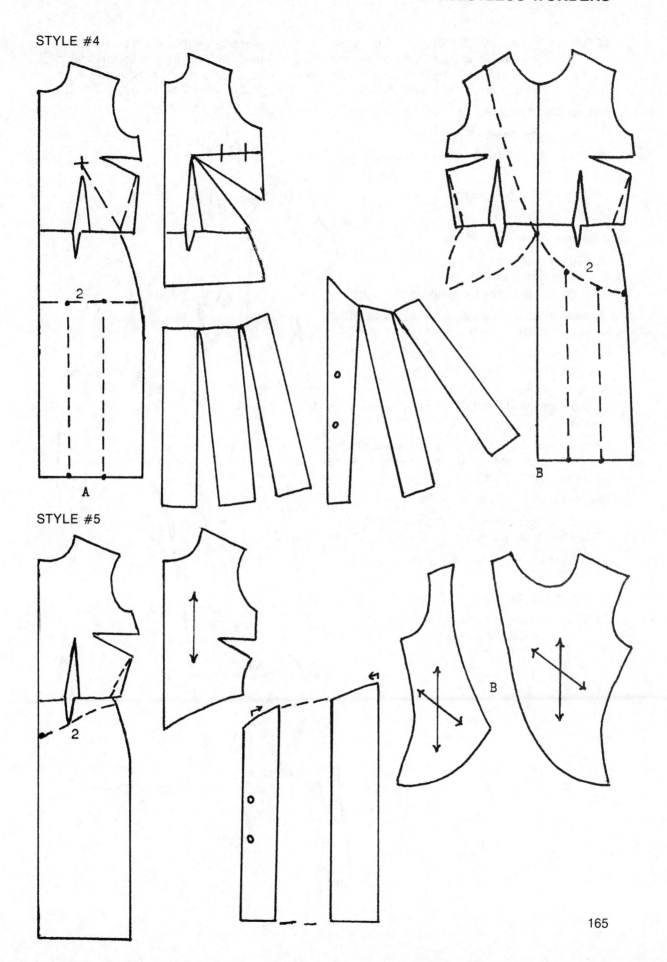

STYLE #5

WAISTLESS WONDERS

STYLE #6 — THE EMPIRE DRESS: This design has many facades, and is always lovely. It is versatile in that it can be made from a variety of fabrics. It is a design that is used frequently in nightgowns and swimsuits. The loose, flowing version can be worn by the fuller figure.

Pattern Construction:

1. Determine design to be used.

2. Follow directions for constructing a one-piece dress.

3. Draw in Empire design.

4. Cut out design.

5. Draw between side and waist darts.

6. Cut and tape side dart. Use upper portion of waist dart for pleats or gathers. Add to bust area for fullness.

7. Lower portion of pattern may be used as a straight sheath or may be A-line.

8. For A-line: Measure from center front to bottom of waist dart. Dot.

9. Measure same amount from center of bottom of skirt. Dot. Draw between dots.

10. Cut and swing together as diagram indicates. Note that you overlap the upper part of dart.

11. Measure yourself under the bust area.

12. Adjust upper part of skirt pattern to the above measurement.

13. You may add additional fullness to side of skirt.

14. Continue design for long skirt.

To Sew: Follow directions from chapter on Gathers, Pleats, Tucks, the Empire Design.

STYLE #6

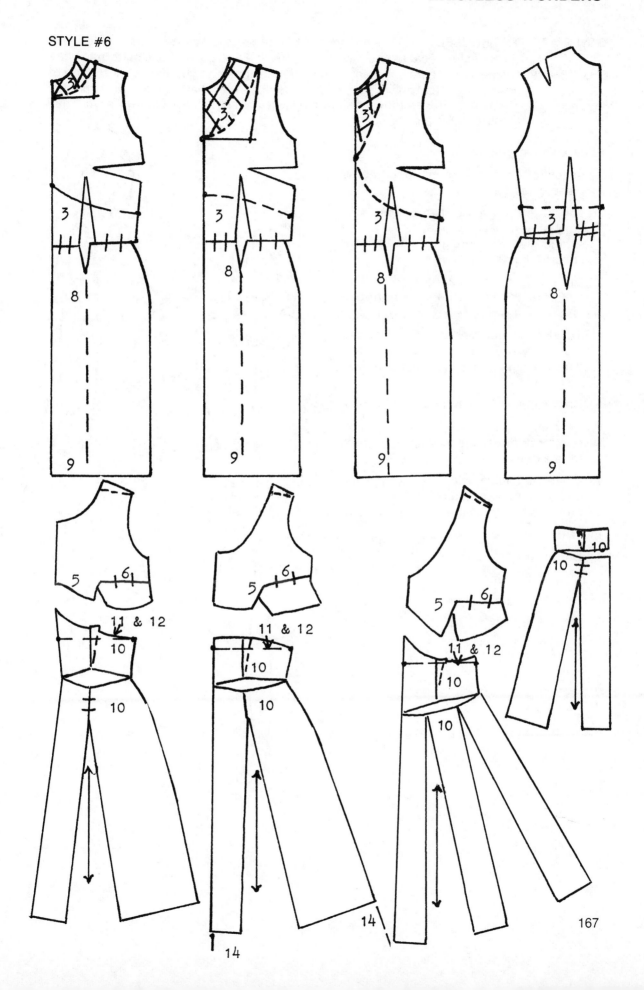

WAISTLESS WONDERS

STYLE #7 — THE HOUSECOAT: The housecoat, of course, is not a dress but is included in this chapter because you have to construct a one-piece dress pattern to work the design. There are many housecoat designs and you can work the top of your design from any of the previous bodice styles that we have constructed. The two examples shown here are basics and are so easy to sew up, you may want to make a dozen.

Pattern Construction:

1. Follow directions for constructing one-piece dress pattern.

2. Lay pattern on top of two opened sections of newspaper and tape down. This should give you enough room for your construction.

3. Draw line from bust dart control to center of shoulder on bodice front pattern.

4. Cut lines — pull side dart together and tape. This throws your dart to the shoulder, which gives a nice lay to the housecoat.

5. Draw sides in to form an A-line.

6. Draw either a front facing onto your pattern for buttons, or add seam allowance for a zipper.

7. A-line the back of your pattern by laying completed front pattern to the back at armhole and tracing outline from front.

FIGURE B:

1. Cut off yoke.

2. Slice to hemline.

3. Close side dart.

4. Straighten side.

STYLE #7

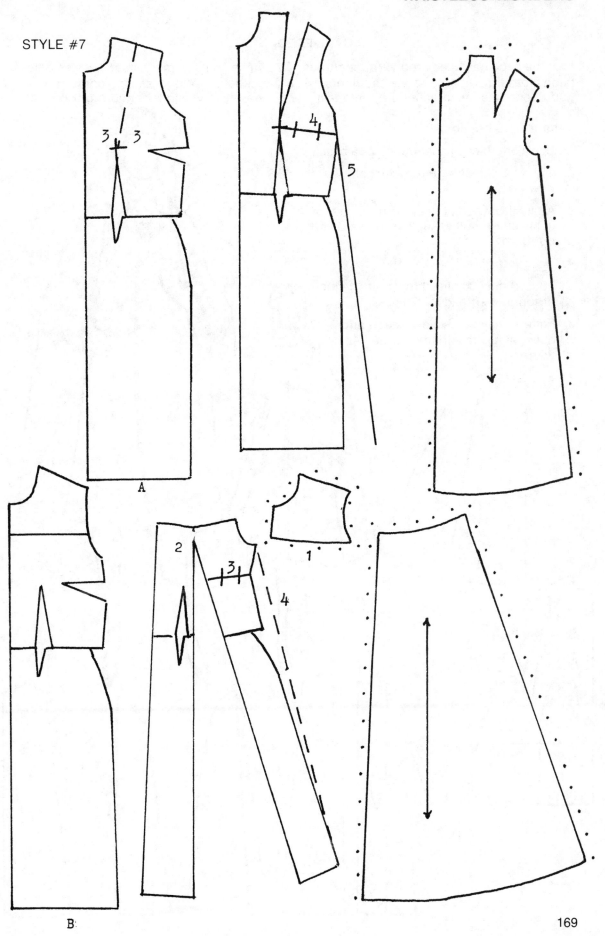

A

B

CAPE ELEGANCE

The cape has been around for centuries. Of course, in its primary stages, it was only a large cloth thrown around the shoulders. Now the cape is cut to follow the contour of the figure, and has taken on a new personality. Below are two versions for you to try.

Pattern Construction:

1. Use a one-piece construction as a basis.

2. Cut your sleeve pattern in half. Turn down cap.

3. Attach front half of sleeve to front pattern at lower armholes. Angle downward and out from side.

4. Repeat for back.

5. Pattern may be sliced to within 1/4 inch of top and spread for fullness.

6. Pattern may be sliced through and pulled apart for princess style. Add fullness.

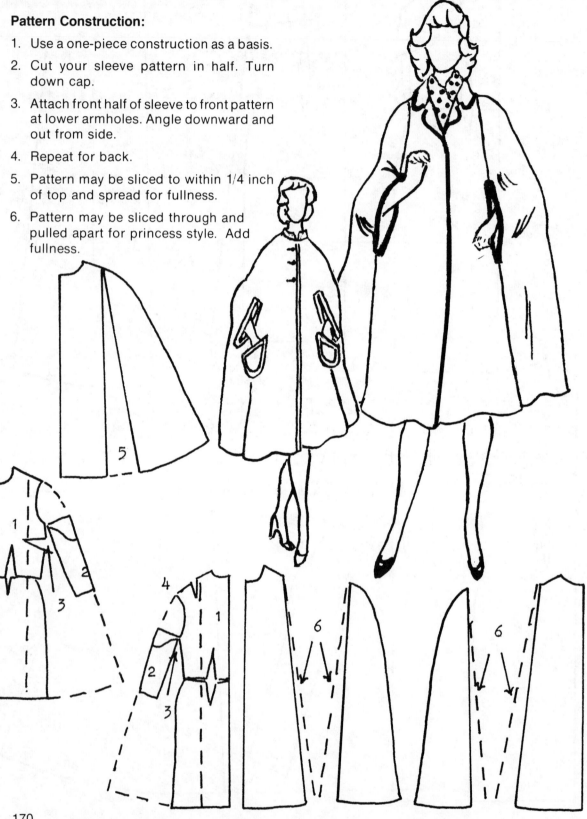

A suit with a well-designed jacket is one item of clothing that is required for a good wardrobe. If you have two suits that have complimentary colors that you can mix and match, you need only a few well-designed blouses in complimentary colors to give you an ample wardrobe. Add a few dresses and slacks and you will have something to wear for any occasion.

To look well, a jacket must fit the individual figure. I recommend that you make your first jacket pattern from Style #1 (A) in this chapter. Draft it onto a trial fabric, something with enough body to simulate the type of fabric that will be used for final jacket (but cheaper). Machine-baste the trial jacket and try on to adjust. No facings are needed for the trial jacket. When you get this one right, you can proceed to the other styles.

Some designers recommend that jacket patterns be split at the beginning of the lapel roll for extra room for collar and lapel turning (see Figures A, B and C). This will work in some figures, but in others (myself included) I find that the opposite is true. Some figures need to have an overlap to the pattern front so that the jacket will lay well on the figure. In fact, this procedure will effect the jacket fit in back as well as in front. Read on.

After you make your trial jacket, stand in front of a mirror and look for these things:

1. Does the jacket have too much ease or too little? Adjust by pinning in or releasing some of the dart or side seam.

2. Does jacket protrude at bottom edge of front? If so, this indicates improper dart control. Try working with the jacket in these areas. With your fingers, pinch up a dart at the side area. Does this take care of the protrusion? If not, pinch jacket at center front either above or below bust. Does this do it? Correct pattern.

3. Stand sideways. Does collar roll-line lie close to the neck? If it pulls away from the neck, it indicates the shoulder blade area of the pattern is too short. Split and lengthen the pattern.

4. Does jacket protrude at the bottom of the back? Believe it or not, but the front of the jacket controls this! Pinch the jacket at center front as you did to test dart control in Step #2 above. Do you see the bottom of jacket swing close to the derriere? If this corrects problem, split pattern front and overlap.

5. Using a hand-mirror, look at the back view of the jacket. Does the jacket lie smoothly in the back with no wrinkles or pulls? If it pulls, jacket is too snug. Split and spread pattern. If it has too much fullness, fold pattern over.

6. If jacket curves up on the derrier, pattern should be curved downward to compensate as directions in this chapter indicate. Check these things with diagrams on page 173.

THE WELL-FITTING JACKET

The hints on the previous pages should help you to have a nice-fitting jacket. Oh yes, there's one other thing. Shoulder pads come and go. Right now they are in, so I should teach you to make your own. Ready-made shoulder pads are expensive and don't fit as well as those that are custom-made.

To adjust the pattern for shoulder pads, determine thickness of pads. Get this right — you don't want your jacket to have the appearance of being too masculine. Some of the new designs make a woman look as if she were trying out for the football team.

Follow directions below for **Custom-Made Shoulder Pads**:

1. Let's say you've decided to use 1/2-inch pads. Then you will add 1/2 inch to the shoulders of your pattern as diagram shows.

2. Add 1/4 to 3/8 inches to armholes.

3. Lay pattern with shoulders touching.

4. Draw shoulder pad onto pattern with 3 inches to the front and 4 to 5 inches to the back, tapering gradually on the back portion. Round off corners.

5. Trace onto a piece of paper. Even-up back shoulder to front.

6. Make two of these patterns. **Use to cut four pad sections. I use heavy-duty pellon for** the pads.

7. Fill with fibrefill, graduating filler to the sides, or decreasing as you work toward the edges. This will eliminate ridges from forming and will give the outside of the jacket a smooth flow. Use tacking stitches to secure pads together.

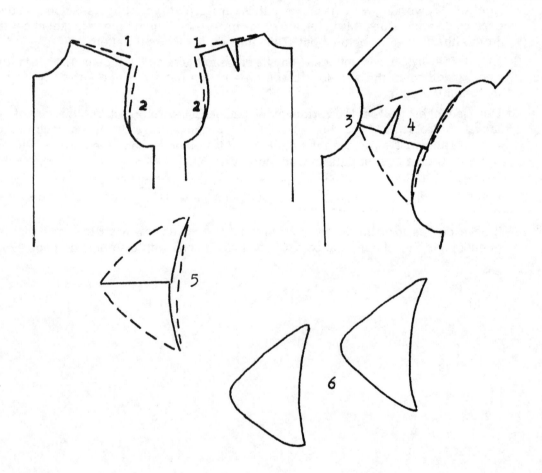

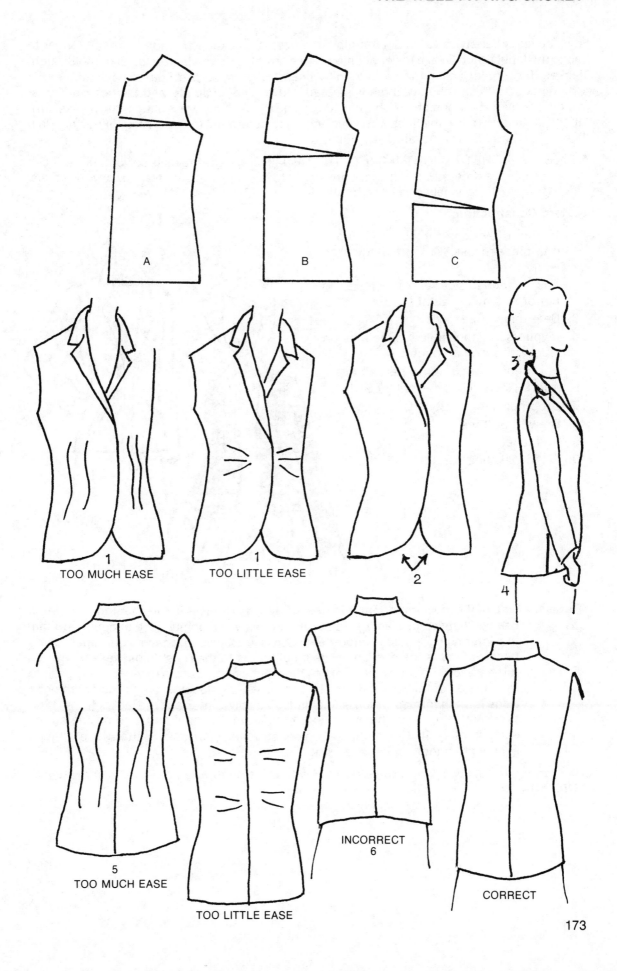

A

B

C

1
TOO MUCH EASE

1
TOO LITTLE EASE

2

3

4

5
TOO MUCH EASE

TOO LITTLE EASE

INCORRECT
6

CORRECT

THE WELL-FITTING JACKET

Jacket collar styles vary. Some follow the normal neckline and some are cut longer to make the lapel notch lie at a lower position. An example is given in Version B of the Straight Jacket. Five collar variations are generally used for jackets: the Shirt, Shawl, Mandarin, Combination (which you have already studied in the collar chapter), and the notched collar which is shown at the end of this chapter. If you see a jacket in a dress shop that you like, turn up the collar and follow the lines with your fingers to determine the cut. Also follow the grain lines. You should have no difficulty doing this.

STYLE #1 — THE STRAIGHT JACKET: This casual, boxy-style jacket is so versatile — it can be dressed up or down, from slacks to evening dresses. Narrow or wide lapels, or no lapels at all can be used.

Pattern Construction:

1. Follow directions for constructing a one-piece dress. Cut off at desired length.
2. Add 1/2 inch to side seams for ease. Do not draw sides straight.*
3. Determine collar style.
4. If you use a lapel, follow directions on lapels from collar chapter.
5. For French dart, refer to dart chapter.
6. Add 1/2 inch to center front for Style A.
7. Drop neckline for Style B.
8. Draw in buttons.
9. Add lapel.
10. Fill in waistline darts.

To Sew: One of the most important features in sewing jackets is in the shaping. I prefer to use two lightweight facings rather than one heavy facing. I'll explain: I find that the interfacing gives a smoother finish if it is placed against the lapel facing because that is the portion of the lapel that is to the outside of the jacket when turned back. This, however, leaves the seams at the button extension exposed to the outside of the jacket without a protective interfacing. When top-stitching, a ridge is often formed which is unsightly. To solve, interface the jacket front. With **two interfacings, you have a smooth finish on the lapel and also on the button extension.** Try it! Remember, when constructing your jacket pattern, use 3/8-inch seams at armhole, neck and front for sewing ease.

Even though you are making a straight jacket, you must give some shape to the side seams. Otherwise, the jacket will be too sloppy looking.

STYLE A

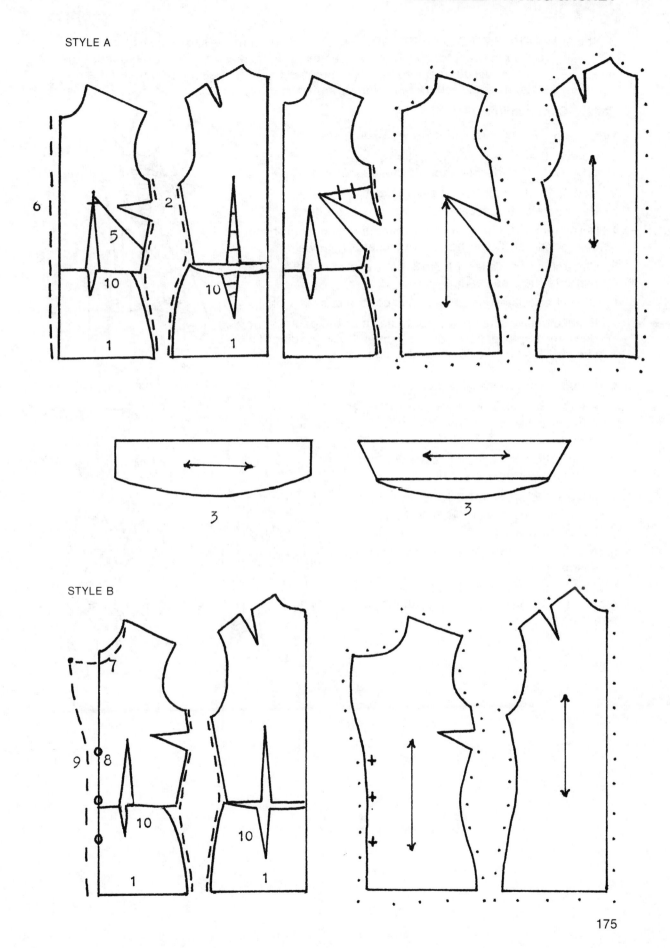

STYLE B

THE WELL-FITTING JACKET

STYLE #2 — THE FITTED JACKET: There are several different ways to make a fitted jacket. You may use dart or princess seams to accomplish this. Four variations are being used to demonstrate. Remember to always use a fabric that has a firm texture for jackets — no flimsy stuff.

Pattern Construction:

Version A – A real easy-fit jacket with some shaping.

1. Follow directions for constructing a one-piece dress pattern. Cut off at desired length. Close side dart.

2. Add 1/4 inch at sides and sleeve sides.

3. Determine button locations — we'll use two here.

4. Determine width of lapel. Follow directions on lapels from collar chapter. Curve bottom of jacket if you wish.

5. Close side dart. Take off 1/2 to 3/4 inch at armhole. Ease the rest into the side seam.

6. Close back dart. Use some of this control at center back.

7. If jackets have a tendency not to lie smooth against your derriere, curve pattern toward center back as diagram shows. This can be done to all jacket patterns.

Version B – The Princess Jacket

1. Follow directions for constructing a one-piece dress pattern. Cut off at desired length.

2. Follow directions on princess style from chapter on princess seams.

3. Determine button locations.

4. Determine lapel style and draw. Curve bottom if desired.

5. Add 1/4 inch to side seams and sleeve seams.

NOTE: To test jacket pattern for lapel correctness, turn back lapel after cutting pattern. See diagram A.

STYLE A

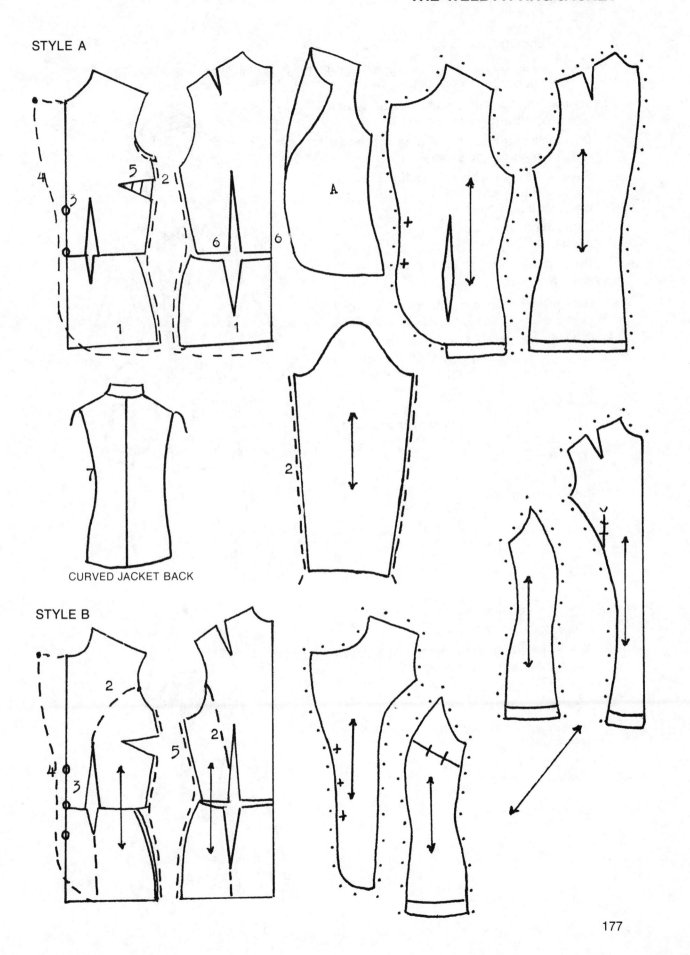

CURVED JACKET BACK

STYLE B

STYLE #2 (cont'd)

Version C – This design eliminates the side seam and puts fit at area close to the arm. It does not fit as snugly as the princess cut, and is also more tailored.

1. Follow directions for a one-piece dress pattern. Cut off at desired length.
2. Draw design for side cut as diagram shows. Add 1/4 inch to side seams.
3. Take 1/2 to 3/4 inch off armhole for dart control. Remaining side dart will be closed when side section is cut.
4. Close back dart. Use some of control at center back.
5. Draw in button location.
6. Draw in lapel extension.
7. Draw line from bottom of bust dart control to hemline.
8. Cut side sections out and close rest of side dart. Tape front and back sections together at sides. Fill in empty space. Move some of side control to each side of new pattern section.
9. Cut line at bottom of bust dart and spread 1 inch. Sew as a dart from under the bust to hemline.
10. Add fly if you wish.
11. Draw collar pattern.

Version D – Another version of the princess.
1. Follow Step #1 above.
2. Follow directions for this princess style from chapter on princess seams.
3. Add 1/4 inch to side seams.
4. Draw button locations.
5. Draw in lapel extension. I'm using a pointed lapel here.
6. Draw collar pattern. Pattern for Version C is used on drawing.

VERSION C

VERSION D

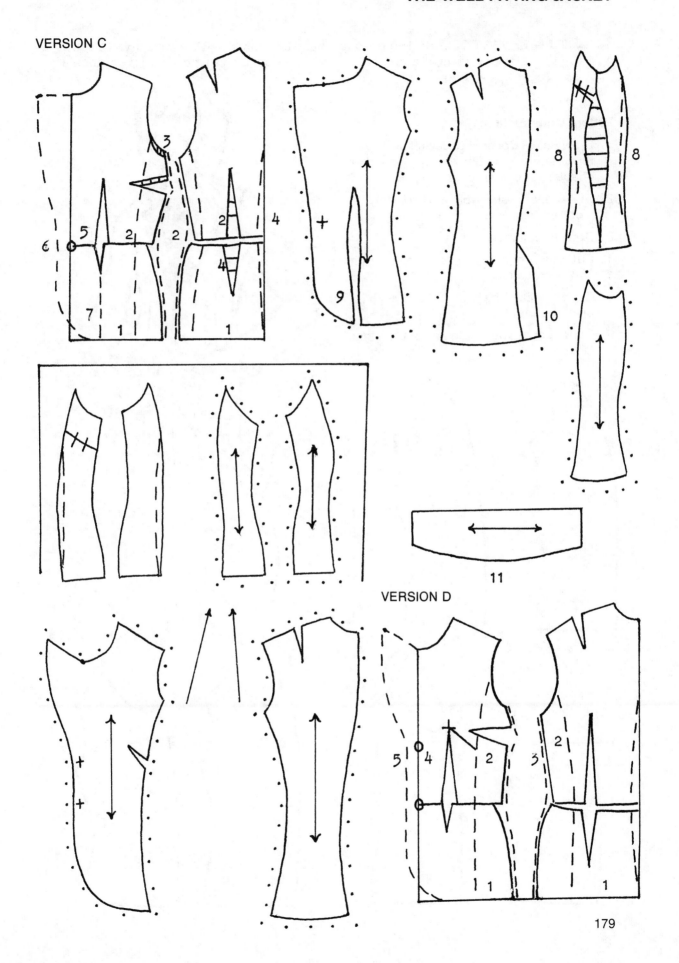

THE WELL-FITTING JACKET

STYLE #3 — SHAWL COLLAR: There is one other jacket that you will want to try. The basis of this jacket lapel and collar is the Shawl Collar. This type of cut is very popular at this writing.

Pattern Construction:

1. Draw Shawl Collar onto Jacket body pattern. Refer to the Shawl Collar in collar chapter for construction.

2. Draw collar design from the two versions pictured below.

3. Draw in collar point.

4. Cut out notch that was formed from above procedure.

5. Cut off collar. The back of collar is to be placed on fold.

6. Construct as you would any of the other jackets.

When something is done right, it is not always noticed, but when it's done wrong, it is. This is especially true in the finishing of a garment. Much time and effort can be put forth to construct a garment but if the finishing is not good, the appeal is just not there. Finishing a garment is that important. A well-turned hem, a zipper with the proper length, curves that look like curves are a must. A touch of lace, top-stitching, buttons, bindings, braid, piping and pockets can change a humdrum garment into one with personality. One important thing to remember: Don't Overdo! To overdo a trim will negate its effectiveness. For instance, notice the two dresses below. The one on the left has the same wide trim at the neck, hem and cuffs — too much!! Now look at the one on the right. The wide trim is used only at the neck. A small edging is used on the cuff at the bottom. This gives more importance to the neck trim and the whole appearance of the dress is more appealing.

Finishing is the final stage and the most important one to get that professional look. If time is of essence to you, forget about finishing the inside to perfection and concentrate on the outside. Look at the ready-mades for the season; see what is being done. Is the top-stitching close to the edge or 1/4 inch over, or are two or three rows of stitching being used? Note other style additions that are being used for finishing. On the following pages we are going to talk about how to do these finishing touches.

The Proper Needle is so important in finishing a garment. Regular Sharps are fine for most sewing. Most knits need a ball point needle. Then there are a few knits that you will find that need a coated needle. Several companies manufacture them. The shaft of the needle is coated; some are yellow, green, blue and copper. The coating keeps the needle cool and permits the needle to sew without skipping stitches. Size of the needle is important too. Use a fine needle for sheers, a medium weight for average fabrics, and a heavy needle for heavy fabrics.

THE FINISHING TOUCH

TOP-STITCHING:

Top-stitching can really add that finishing touch to a garment. Most home sewers make the mistake of using stitches that are too small. Top-stitching is not used to secure the garment so, therefore, does not have to be small. Look at some of the ready-mades and adjust your top-stitching accordingly. I find that using two threads in the needle gives a much better effect on the heavier fabrics.

It is very important to keep your top-stitching straight. You may have your own method but, if not, I will pass on a few hints that may help. I use my zigzag presser foot to give me three different top-stitching widths. For 1/4-inch top-stitching, needle position will be at center and edge of presser foot will be even with the edge of garment. For 1/8-inch top-stitching, switch needle position to the right with your needle adjusting knob. For 3/8-inch top-stitching, switch needle position to the left. For anything wider, you must use a gauge. If you don't have one, use scotch tape as a guide. Just tape to the machine with the left edge of the tape to be used as a guide.

PIPING:

It is very difficult to find piping in the right color and texture for most of your garments, so I'll tell you how to do your own. Buy a good grade of wrapping twine that has firm edges. Cut off several yards and shrink by washing. Keep handy for future use.

To cover the twine for piping, you will cut strips of bias fabric either in the fabric of your garment or a corresponding one. Cut bias strips 1 inch wide and as long as you can get out of your fabric. If you have to piece, try to apply in the most inconspicuous place when you sew onto garment. If you are using lightweight fabric, you will need to double the width of your strips and fold over before sewing to twine. Fold bias strips over the twine and, using your zipper foot, sew with a large stitch as close to the twine as possible. It is now ready to apply to garment. Remember though, when you apply piping around a curve, work loosely and clip the piping every half-inch. This allows the piping to lay smoothly.

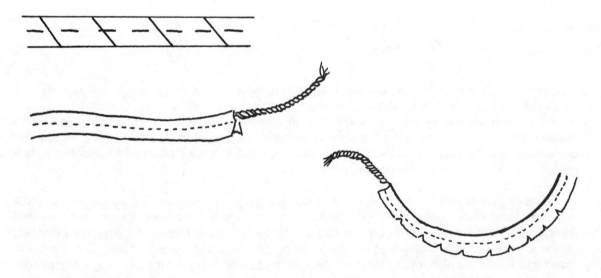

CURVES:

Curves are a tell-tale sign of a "home-made" garment. Most sewers have not mastered sewing smooth curves. Really, it is not difficult to master. You do have to be conscientious — curves can be puzzling. When you sew what you think is a beautiful curve and then turn it, most of the time you find that it looks very much unlike a curve. So, what you have to do is learn to exaggerate shallowing a curve. For instance, if you want the finished curve to look like this:

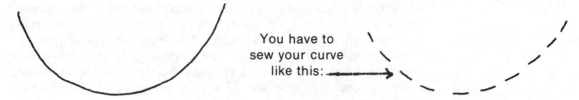

You have to sew your curve like this: ⟶

Trimming curves is also important. You must trim very closely for the curves to look smooth, so be sure to stitch twice to secure seams. When sewing curved pockets, it is best to line them. It is very difficult to sew on a pocket, curving the seams as you sew when the pocket is not lined. Master this!

POINTS:

Below are some examples of points that most sewers have difficulty with. They will sometimes pucker or will not look pointed after the garment is turned.

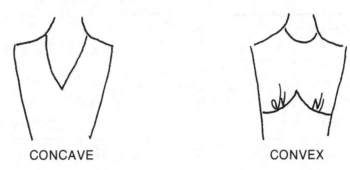

CONCAVE   CONVEX

To get a concave point to look well, it is best to sew away from the point in both directions. This distributes the fabric evenly and eliminates puckering. For the convex point, you sew the same; but if the point is very sharp (as it sometimes is when making a dress with a midriff that extends between the bust), it is difficult to obtain. To handle this type of point, sew 1/2 inch from point outward on both sides. Turn the garment to right side and with the fingers, form the point. Pin and tack, by hand, from underneath. Good luck!

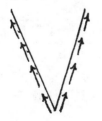
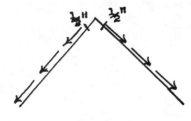

BINDING:

To bind a garment, you can use commercial binding or you can make your own. You can usually get better color coordination by making your own. Here's how.

Let's say that you want your finished binding to be 1/2 inch. You will cut 3-inch bias strips from your fabric as long as possible (piece if you have to). Fold the strips over and press. Stay-stitch 1/4 inch from cut edge — this will be the edge you will sew to the garment. To prepare garment, cut off seam allowance where the binding is to be attached. If you will have facings, they are to be cut off too. Stay-stitch facing and garment together close to edge. Pin binding to edge of garment. Stitch on stay-stitching line of binding. When pinning, do not stretch binding. On the convex curves (around bottom of jacket and curved pockets, etc.) you will need to ease the binding so you will have sufficient fabric to work around the curves. On the concave curves (armholes, U-necks, round necks, etc.) you need to stretch the binding a little. This will keep the binding from looking ripply when you work the binding over the edges.

To complete, turn the folded edge of the binding over the seam edge and pin every inch. Now, stitch on top close to binding. This is called *Stitching in the Ditch* because you're actually stitching where the binding joins the garment. Turn and press. You can't even see your stitches, can you?

TRIM SEAMS
SEW 1/4 INCH
FROM EDGE

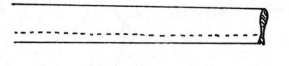

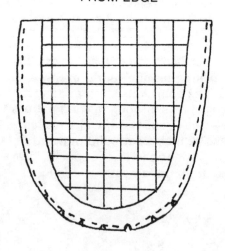

CLIP CURVES

TURN AND PIN

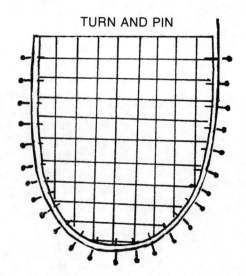

STITCH IN THE DITCH

WHAT ABOUT HEMS?

Sometimes I see a well-made garment only to look down and see a hem with all the stitches showing, or bulging, or maybe the hem is just too wide. A well-turned hem is not hard to do. It's just knowing how to do it.

A hem should not be more than 2-1/2 inches on a straight skirt. A hem that is too wide is unattractive. An A-line or circular skirt will need less. Average for an A-line is 1 to 1-1/2 inches, depending on how much flare the skirt has. A circular skirt does better with a 1/4-inch hem. If you try to put too much hem in a skirt with flare, you end up with bunching at the hemline.

Here's how to do it properly:

You will use the catch-stitch, which allows you to cross over from hem to garment without securing the two together. This is the secret of the smooth look to the outside. There is no binding when it is done this way. The hem is completely free of the garment. You must pick up only a thread or two with the needle when you stitch on the garment side. Each stitch must be secured by back-stitching. Try not to turn under the edge of the hem as this creates bulk. If at all possible, zigzag the edge of the hem before hemming. This will keep the edge from raveling. If you use lace, you must use an easing stitch on the edge of the hem before applying lace. This will allow you to pull the hem to fit the part of the garment that it will lay against; otherwise, the lace will bunch as you hem.

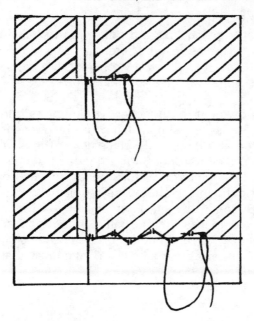

Step #1 — Secure first stitch at the side seam, stitching the hem to the side seam.

Step #2 — Pick up one or two threads on the garment using back-stitch.

Step #3 — Cross over to the hem and pick up the edge of the hem with a back-stitch.

Step #4 — Repeat until hem is completed.

THE FINISHING TOUCH

INTERFACINGS:

Interfacings are so very important in making your garment look professional. It is difficult to get a good interfacing, especially for knits. So many of the pellon interfacings wrinkle under the garment and show through. Also I find that interfacings are very expensive. Many times I find that it is possible to use the fabric with which you are sewing your garment to use for interfacing. A good heavy cotton also makes a good interfacing, but should be cut on the bias so that it rolls well with the collar or lapel. For shirts, a product called *"Shirtmaker"* is excellent. It gives a crisp look and holds up through washing, and it does not wrinkle. Gabardine is an excellent interfacing for heavier fabrics. Sheer fabric, such as that used in sheer curtains, is excellent for lightweight fabrics. Start looking through all that fabric that you've got stored away and see what kind of goodies you can come up with.

In applying interfacing, you will get better results by applying to the upper collar and lapel. When you do this, the seams are turned under the interfacing and this leaves the outside of the garment nice and smooth. If the garment has a front opening, you will also need to use a 1-1/2-inch strip of interfacing against the garment as well (to cover the seams) because the lapel interfacing won't take care of this. Remember: Get those seams under an interfacing for a smooth, professional look!

Many times I use two lightweight interfacings rather one heavy; I get better results this way. I interface the upper and lower collar, the lapel and the dress or jacket front. Try it!

Since I'm only giving tips and not trying to teach sewing, actual application will not be covered here. I assume you already know how to apply interfacings. If you need help, there are several excellent sewing books that will give you this information.

BUTTONS & BUTTON HOLES:

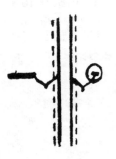

To finish a garment to perfection, it is important to place buttons properly. It's easy to distinguish a couturier garment just by looking at the button and buttonhole placement. There will always be an adequate extension from button to edge of garment. The rule is: Button size determines the width of space from the edge of the button to edge of garment. It should be the same width as the button. *Example:* Button = 1 inch; Extension = 1-1/2 inch. You add the half-inch to compensate for the half of the button that extends over to the extension. The buttonholes will be the same distance from the edge as the buttons but will be wider, of course, than the buttons to allow for buttoning.

WHAT ABOUT ZIPPERS?

Zippers are a necessary item for a fitted dress but (with the exception of a front, decorative zipper) they should be as inconspicuous as possible.

A mistake is often made of sewing in a zipper that is too long or too short. To create a uniform effect, the right length of zipper should be as follows:

WRONG
TOO LONG

WRONG
TOO SHORT

RIGHT
JUST RIGHT

The zipper at the left comes below the hipline and seems to be just dangling. The one in the middle stops above the hipline and seems to point to the hips. The one at the right comes just to the hipline and seems to blend right in.

Zippers can be sewn in two ways:

LAP   EVEN

To sew zippers: If it is hard for you to sew straight, press down the seam allowance at the zipper opening. Lay zipper opening with right side up on a table. Using tailors' chalk and a tape, dot your sewing line. For a lap zipper, the left side will be dotted 1/2 inch from the folded edge. For an even zipper, 1/4 inch is best. Now draw a straight line with a ruler, using your dots to guide you. Pin zipper in and sew on drawn lines.

To sew zippers by hand: I use this method for sewing in zippers, with the exception of tailored garments. Follow above directions but, instead of stitching on machine, use a back-stitch and make stitches 1/4 inch apart. It's really beautiful and lies down so much better.

THE FINISHING TOUCH

COLOR COORDINATING: An effective way to achieve a designer look is learning to combine colors that compliment. You know all the usual ones — navy-red-white, etc. — but how about these:

Navy-white-fuchsia . . . navy-beige-red . . . light blue-lemon yellow-white . . . darkest burgundy-palest pink . . . purple-aqua . . . brown-tan-burnt orange . . . brown-white-amber . . . peach-bone-rust . . . fuchsia-red . . . purple-red . . . green-lavender . . . green-pink . . . royal blue-green . . . royal blue-aqua . . . grey-navy-purple . . . purple-blue . . . pale orange-pink . . . pink-tan-brown.

Three hues of the same color range are stunning. So are colors that are in the same color hue but contrast sharply as the lightest and the darkest of the color hue.

You must remember that even though mixing unusual colors can be effective, the right hue combination is important. Test for eye-appeal. Lay the colors out for awhile; let your eyes become accustomed to them. If you like to look at them, they're probably right together. They should be eye-appealing.

POCKETS AND MORE

Pockets were first used as a functional item of a garment, but now they are also used as a designer's touch. They can really add personality to a garment to give that distinctive custom look.

There are two basic kinds of pockets: patch pockets and set-in pockets. The patch pocket is sewn on the outside of the garment while the functional part of the set-in pocket is sewn inside the garment. Only a flap or welt appears on the outside. I often use the set-in pocket flap or welt for effect on a garment, but eliminate the set-in portion because I never use it. I'll show you how to make "fake pockets" in this chapter.

Most sewers make a mistake in positioning the pocket. Most have a tendency to place hip pockets too low or too close to the center of a garment. Remember, get them over to the sides where they belong. Another mistake is to make pockets too large or too small; large pockets will overpower a small frame while too-small pockets on a large frame looks ridiculous.

I find that it's best (although a little harder) to sew pockets onto the garment last. This way, you can try on the dress, jacket, etc., and pin the pockets on just where they appear to be right. Of course, you can't always do this with a set-in pocket, so be very careful as you apply these. You just have one chance to get it right as you have to slice the garment to apply these pockets.

Pockets, in most cases, look better if they are lined. If they are to be applied to suit jackets, coats or dresses of a fabric that is suit weight, they lay better if they are also interfaced.

In this chapter we will cover various pockets and their construction. We will also cover pocket flaps, tabs, ties and buttonholes.

PATCH POCKETS: Patch pockets can be squared, rounded or pointed. Below are some illustrations of patch pockets:

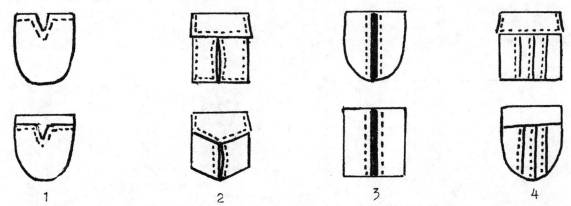

1   2   3   4

The figure size will determine pocket size. Average figure will require a 5- to 6-inch patch pocket for suit jackets. For an average man, the pocket will be 6-3/4 to 8 inches. Average breast pockets run 4 to 4-1/2 inches for women and 4-1/2 to 5-1/2 inches for men. Cut your pattern on paper but try out on muslin for effect.

Version #1

Cut square of paper the width and depth you desire pocket to be. Fold in half and round off bottom. Clip center top for style indention. For inset: Cut off top of pattern before clipping. Make pattern for inset 4 inches by width of pattern. This will be folded at top to make 2-inch inset. One-half inch will be above pocket.

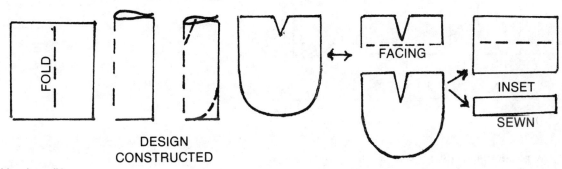

DESIGN CONSTRUCTED

FACING

INSET

SEWN

Version #2

Cut square of paper the width and depth you want; fold in half and cut for point if desired. Cut pattern in half and fill in with 2-1/2-inch strip of paper for inverted pleat. Pocket flaps should be 1/4 inch wider than pocket for smooth overlay.

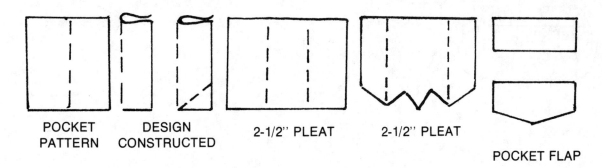

POCKET   DESIGN
PATTERN   CONSTRUCTED   2-1/2" PLEAT   2-1/2" PLEAT

POCKET FLAP

189

POCKETS AND MORE

Version #3

Cut square of paper the width and depth you want. Cut out 1/2-inch strip from center of pattern. Add 3/4-inch seams to centers. Make contrasting fill-in 2 inches wide by depth pattern. Turn down seam allowance and add fill-in to get idea of finished product. The two sides will be top-stitched to the fill-in 1/2 inch from edge of folded sections.

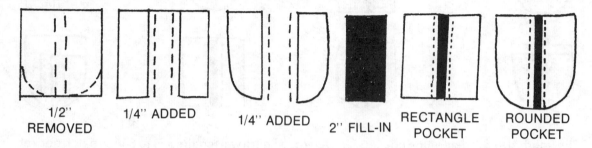

| 1/2"
REMOVED | 1/4" ADDED | 1/4" ADDED | 2" FILL-IN | RECTANGLE
POCKET | ROUNDED
POCKET |

Version #4

Cut square of paper the width and depth you want. Fold in half and round off bottom. Cut off band portion. Slice bottom of pattern in half. Insert strip 3/4 inch wide — this will be distributed evenly between three tucks. Double band, and add seam allowance so that it can be folded to make facing. If you use a pocket flap, add 1/4 inch to width of flap.

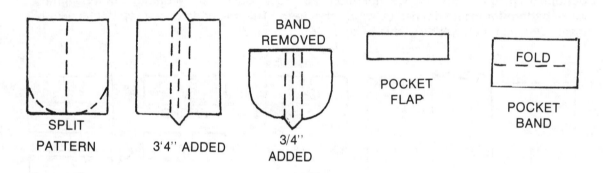

SPLIT PATTERN   3'4" ADDED   BAND REMOVED 3/4" ADDED   POCKET FLAP   POCKET BAND

Version #5

I have often used this pocket on little girls' dresses. Cut paper pattern the width and depth you wish pocket to be. Slice pattern from top to within 1/4 inch of bottom. Spread to desired fullness. You may make a band for the top or gather 3/4 inch below top for ruffle. I do not line this pocket but use only 1/4-inch seam — this helps to make pocket nice and round.

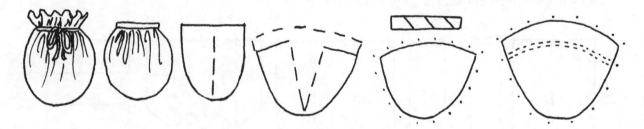

Version #6

This pattern is for patch pockets to be used on skirts or slacks. Cut paper length and width you wish. Angle or curve side as diagram shows, leaving 1 to 1-1/2 inches at top and 3 to 4 inches at side. The side of the pocket works into side seam of skirt or slacks so, if skirt is A-line, pocket will also have same shape on the side as the skirt. Top sews into waistband. An extension may be made at the top the same width as pocket top to be used as belt loops.

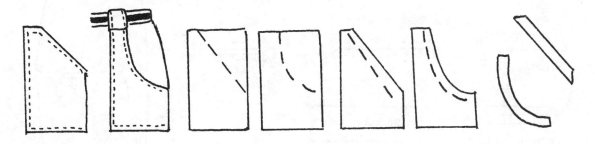

FAKE INSET POCKETS:

Flap Style: Make flap any style you wish. Sew flaps to pocket position. Zigzag over raw edge to eliminate bulk. Turn down and press. Tack ends 1/2 inch at top.

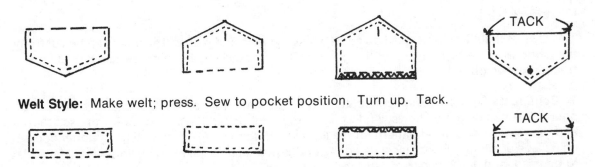

Welt Style: Make welt; press. Sew to pocket position. Turn up. Tack.

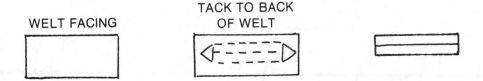

Double Welt Style: Follow directions for Version #2 of the inset pockets on the following page but, instead of using the insets, just take a piece of fabric 2 inches in depth and 1 inch longer than pocket welts (finished) and tack this section behind the welts to take the place of the pocket.

WELT FACING

TACK TO BACK
OF WELT

Slanted Hip Pocket: Draw design onto pattern. Cut. Add 1-1/2 inches to each side. To sew, turn under seam of upper pocket. Top-stitch to other section to get pocket look.

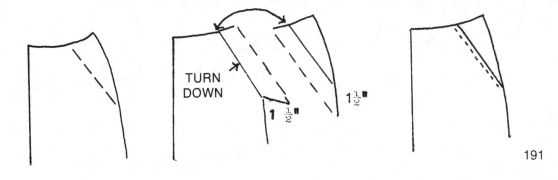

TURN
DOWN

1   $1\frac{1}{2}$"

$1\frac{1}{2}$"

Version #2

This is sewn as in Version #1 with the exception that the welt is sewn to the lower part of the slice. If it is to be used on an angled pocket, one side of the inside pocket will be longer than the other. For double welt: Follow directions for bound buttonholes. Then sew insets onto welt. Complete as above.

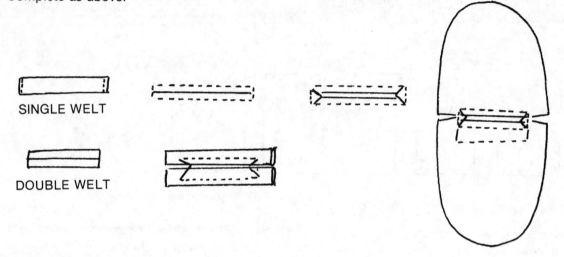

Version #3

This style of **Inset Pocket** is used on coats, jackets, skirts and pants. The inset can be cut from the fabric which is being used for the garment if it is not too heavy. Otherwise, it must be cut from a lightweight fabric.

To Construct: (1) Draw design onto pattern. (2) Cut apart. (3) For self-fabric, add remainder of pocket inset as diagram shows. (4) For lightweight fabric, add 1-1/2 inches for the self-fabric and use remainder of inset pattern for the lightweight fabric. (5) Trace outline of upper pocket on a piece of paper. (6) Add inset using the under-pocket as a guide. (7) If lightweight fabric is to be used, add 1-1/2 inches of self-fabric at the top.

To Sew: Whenever I can't use self-fabric for this pocket, I cut the entire pocket out of the lightweight fabric and then add the self-fabric portions on top of the pockets. If tab or flap is being used, sew these to upper pocket before sewing pocket facing to upper pocket.

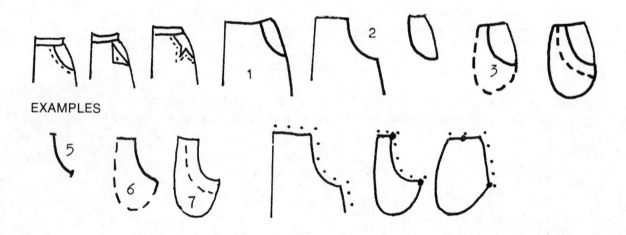

EXAMPLES

THE SET-IN POCKET: Below are several illustrations of set-in pockets:

Make pocket flap from directions below. (1) Mark location of pocket on garment. (2) Top-stitch a rectangle the width of the flap and 1/4 inch wide. (3) Reinforce with second stitching just inside the first. (4) Clip to corners. (5) Sew flap to upper part of slice with underside facing you. (6) Cut two pocket sections the same size. This saves confusion in sewing. You can even them up later. (7) Sew one section over flap. (8) Sew other section to bottom of slice. Turn both sections to inside of garment. (9) Sew pocket sections together, catching the ends of the clipped slice with the lower section of the inside pocket as you sew. As you can see, one portion of inside pocket is lower than the other. Trim off.

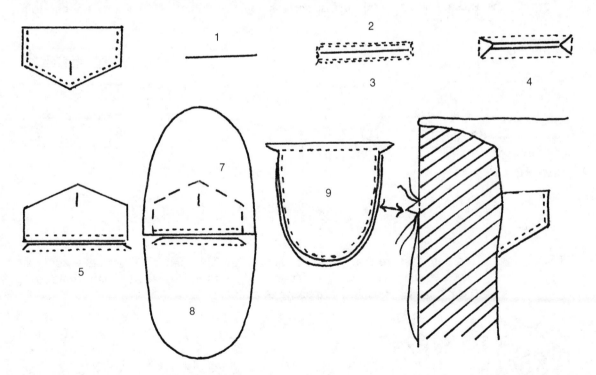

Pocket Flaps: Flaps can dress up a pocket and they are easy to make. The flap should be 1/4 inch wider than the pocket so that it will ride well over the pocket. They average 1-1/2 to 2-1/2 inches in depth. **To Construct:** Follow directions for patch pocket but shorten in depth.
To Sew: Sew flaps 1/2 inch above pocket to allow space for hand to enter pocket.

POCKETS AND MORE

THE TAB: Below can be seen the various ways that tabs are used to enhance a garment. Maybe you can think of other ways.

There are two methods for making tabs:

A. (1) Cut pattern the length and width you wish. (2) Fold in half and cut pointed end. Use interfacing when you sew together.

B. (1) Cut pattern the length and width you wish. Do not cut points. Double pattern so that you have only one seam. **To Sew:** (2) Fold over tab and sew seams together. Do not sew end. (3) Turn and press so that the seam is in the center of the underside. (4) Fold unsewn ends together with seam side out. (5) Turn and press point into place. If you wish a deeper point, sew the end at a slant.

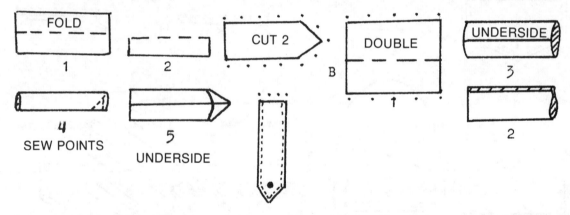

TIES: Ties can be a real addition to garments. Ties can be used as accents on necklines, sleeves, waists and hiplines. They range in size from a thin bias string to a big bow tie. Below are some examples:

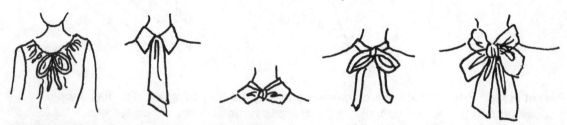

Bias String Tie: Cut bias strip of fabric as long as you wish and 1-1/2 inches wide. You may have to piece. Fold in half and sew 3/8 inch from the fold. Turn, do not press. This tie shouldn't lie flat. Knot ends or turn inside and tack.

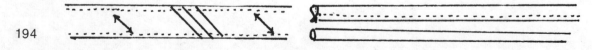

Bow Tie: Determine width: 2-1/2 inches is good. Using a piece of fabric 5 inches wide (plus seam) and 60 inches (give or take a few inches), cut either on the bias or straight of grain. You probably will have to piece fabric to get this length. If so, place the seam either at the back of the neck or at the neckline center front. Fold and sew, making ends either straight or pointed. You may want to flare the ends of the tie. Leave portion in middle to sew to neckline. I give one side of the tie 4 inches more than the other; then when you tie the bow, the ends hang evenly. This tie folds over at neckline to form mandarin-type collar.

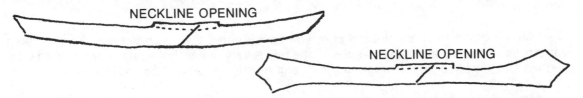

Knotted Tie: This tie is sewn onto a straight mandarin collar and ties into a smart single bow. Cut bow sections 6 inches long (plus seam) and 2 inches wide. Fold and sew. Ends may be straight or pointed. Gather ends to sew to mandarin.

BOUND BUTTONHOLES: Bound buttonholes are much neater if they are made in two sections.

(1) Mark buttonholes on garment. (2) Determine width and size of welt. Let's say our buttonholes will be 1-1/2 inches wide and the welts 1/4 inch wide. (3) Use a piece of fabric about 3 inches wide and 12 inches long, and cut iron-on interfacing the same. (4) Press together. (5) Cut welt strips from this: 2 inches by 1 inch. (6) Fold welts in half and press. (7) Lay two welts on each buttonhole with raw edges together. (8) Tape down with scotch tape. (9) Sew down middle of welts. (10) Remove tape and sew again to secure. *Do not sew ends.* (11) Turn garment over to wrong side. (12) Clip buttonholes. (13) Pull welts to wrong side. (14) Sew raw ends of buttonhole to welt, keeping seams straight. (15) You will have to do this step after all buttonholes are made: Sew facing to garment. (16) Mark on facing from buttonhole side. Clip and whip facing to buttonhole.

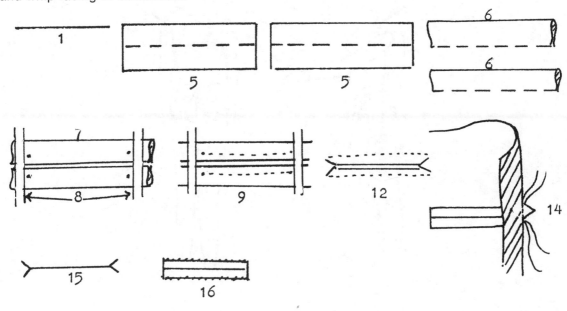

HOW TO DRAFT YOUR OWN BASIC PATTERN

When I first began designing my own patterns, I used a basic commercial pattern but was unhappy with it because it just wasn't a good fit. I didn't know what was wrong. There were so many things that needed adjusting it just seemed hopeless. I really started thinking about it one day and decided that if a house could be built from a blueprint, then a blueprint could be made for the body. Using geometric angles, I started to experiment. The first pattern wasn't very good but it gave me hope. Over the years I have perfected it to the point where I can get a near perfect pattern the first time I draft one. The few bugs present are corrected in the muslin pattern. You can do it too!

You are going to be so pleased after you have drafted your own pattern. To draft your pattern, you need a good tape measure — one that is very flexible. You also need a good ruler and yardstick, newsprint for rough drafting, and muslin for perfecting your pattern.

After you rough-draft your pattern, you will transfer to muslin, sew it up, try it on, make adjustments (a friend or husband comes in handy here) and draft it onto something permanent.

Better fit is accomplished by measuring the bodice front and back separately which you will do when you make your basic pattern. Before you begin to measure, you will need to do the following:

1. Tie a string belt around your waist.

2. Using colored chalk, divide your body on the sides so that your body looks symmetrical. Center shoulders and draw line.

3. Place a pin at the tip of your bra on both sides.

4. Square off your neck with a ball-point pen (one that washes off).

5. Draw around your arms (at the point where they join the body).

Now you are ready to begin measuring!

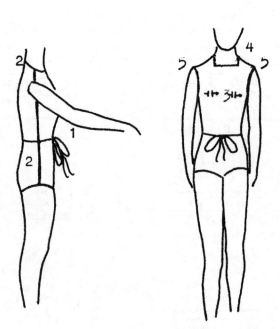

All horizontal measurements will be made from chalk lines drawn at sides to separate body.

BODICE FRONT

Measure the following:

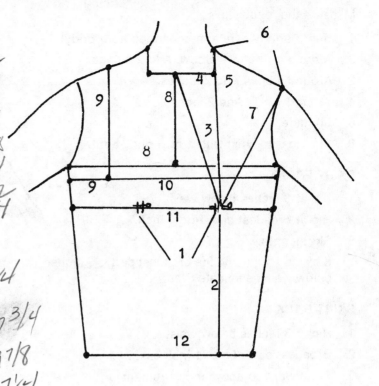

1. Bust width (pin to pin). 8 3/8
2. Bust to waist. 4 1/2   7 3/4
3. Bust to center neck.
4. Horizontal line at neck. 5 1/4
5. Shoulder-neck to bust. 10 5/8
6. Shoulder (add 1/4 inch). 5 3/4
7. Shoulder-arm to bust. 10 1/2
8. Across chest (where arms separate from body, and also from this line to center neck (no ease). 14
9. Center shoulder to 1 inch below chest line, and across to side. 8 1/4
10. Underarm line: located at above dot (add 1/4-inch ease). 17 3/4
11. Bust (add 1/2-inch ease). 19 7/8
12. Waist (add 1/4-inch ease). 17 1/4

BODICE BACK

Measure the following:

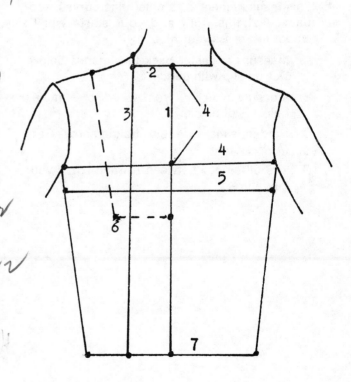

1. Neck to waist. 14
2. Horizontal line at neck. 6 3/4
3. Shoulder-neck to waist. 15 1/4
4. Shoulder blades (where arms separate from body). 14 Measure distance from neck. 5 5/8
5. Underarm, approximately 1-1/2 inches below line above (add 1/2-inch ease). 18 1/2
6. Dart location for lower back. This will be between 3 to 4 inches from center back, and at a slight angle from center shoulder. Measure to center back line. 13 1/2
7. Waist (add 1/4-inch ease). 17 3/4

BODY MEASUREMENTS

ARM

Measure the following:

1. Upper arm (where arm separates from body). 12³/₄
2. Around arm above elbow. Add 2 inches. 15
3. Around elbow. Add 2 inches. 14
4. Around wrist. Add 2 inches. 8³/₄
5. Shoulder to elbow. 14
6. Shoulder to wrist with arm slightly bent. 24¹/₄

SKIRT FRONT

1. Hip at 3 inches below waist. 21
2. Hip at broadest part. Add 1 inch. 23³/₈
3. Skirt length. 28

   If hips are high and the broadest part is 3 inches below waist, eliminate Step #2.

SKIRT BACK

1. Hip at 3 inches below waist. 20
2. Broadest part of hip (1-inch ease). 25³/₄
3. From waist to above measurement. 11
4. This measurement is to determine curvature of back. Get this right and your skirts will fit smoothly across your hips:

   A. Measure at center back to 3 inches below. Dot on slip with pencil.

   B. Measure side hip from waist to 3 inches below. Dot on slip.

   C. Hold tape measure very straight across from 9³/₄ (A) to side hip.

   D. The difference between (B) and (C) is your 2¼ curvature. (1¼)

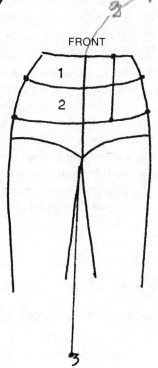

FRONT

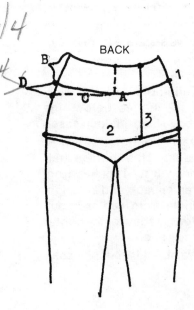

BACK

198

SKIRT BACK (cont'd)

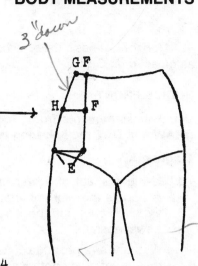

3" down

5. This measurement determines your hip curve.

   E. Measure 3 inches from side hip at broadest part. Dot.

   F. Lay tape measure straight up from the above dot. Dot at waist and again at 3 inches below. 14

   G. Measure from side at waist to dot. 14

   H. Measure from side to dot at 3 inches. 10

PANT FRONT

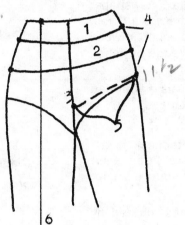

1. Three inches below waist. 20

2. Six inches below waist. 21 7/8

3. Waist to point where body curves under at stride. 12

4. Find panty line. Dot. Measure (generally 6-1/2 to 8 inches from waist). 8 7/8

5. Point body curves under to dot at panty line.

6. Waist to top of shoe. 43

11 1/2

PANT BACK

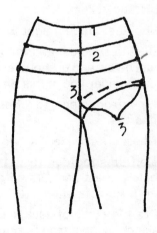

1. Three inches below waist.

2. Six inches below waist. 23 7/8

3. Point body curves under to dot at panty line. 14"

4. Entire stride from waist in front to waist at back. *No ease.* 35"

PATTERN IN THE ROUGH

Horizontal lines must be divided by two in drafting a half-pattern. Vertical lines will be used as measured. On the facing page are diagrams which you will follow.

BODICE FRONT

Using measurements from Body Chart, DRAW and DOT the following lines:

Diagram A

0. Using a sheet of newspaper, cut a rectangle the width of your bust (divided by two) and the length of the newspaper. 4 5/16

1. With one straight edge of newspaper to your left and another toward you, draw bust width, #1 on chart (divided by two) at the lower edge of paper. Draw from left to right.

2. From waist to bust. This is your dart control point. Important.

3. Draw in line for bust.

4. Line from bust to center neck. Measurement will fall naturally on the left edge of the paper where it's supposed to.

5. Horizontal line at neck, divided by two.

6. Draw vertical line, to connect to line above, 4 inches long.

7. Bust to shoulder. Will fall naturally on the above line.

8. Shoulder line. Straight for now.

9. Bust to shoulder at armhole. Locate just below end of shoulder line. Draw in shoulder line at this time.

10. Line from neck to chest (#8 on chart).

11. Chest line, divided by two.

12. Center shoulder to 1-1/2 inches below chest line. Draw from this to right side of pattern.

13. Draw in curve of neck. It's easier to sketch a curve than to draw one unbroken line.

14. From shoulder to line #12 above.

You will draw through chest line dot (#11 above).

15. Cut out pattern neck, shoulder and arm area. See Diagram B.

Diagram B

16. Waist measurement, divided by two.

17. Difference between waistline and side. This is amount of dart control you have.

18. Divide dart control. Give 3/4 inch to side. Cut off.

19. Give about one-third of remainder to side dart (located on bust line) and two-thirds to waist dart. Divide equally on each side of waist dart. Cut out both darts.

Diagram C

20. There is an area between the dart control point and the armhole that needs dart control for pattern to fit properly. Slice pattern from armhole to control point as diagram shows. Overlap 1/2 inch for small bust, up to 1 inch for large bust. This, as you see, has made the side dart larger, which is actually where the control will be taken care of.

21. The bust dart is thrown too high by the above procedure. Relocate dart as diagram shows. See 21-A. Tape dart, 21-B.

22. Draw underarm line at end of center shoulder line, divided by two. Cut off excess from armhole to side dart. See 22-A.

23. Tape a piece of paper under armhole. Draw armhole curve. This gives needed ease for chestline.

Pattern is ready to be drafted onto muslin.

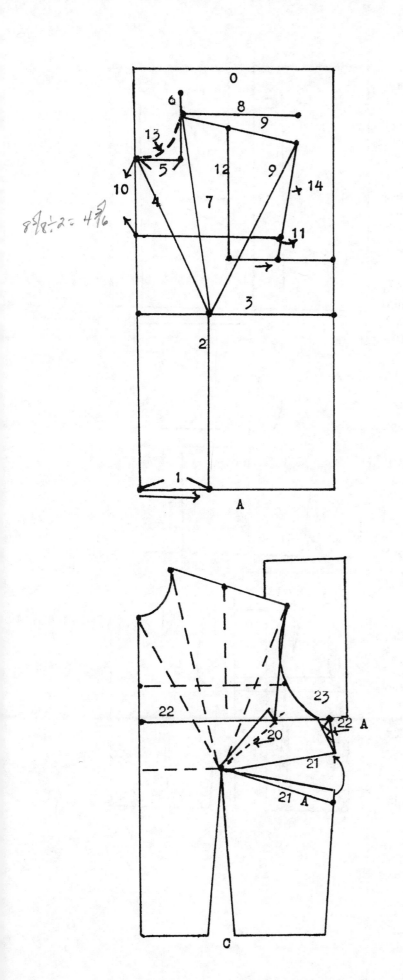

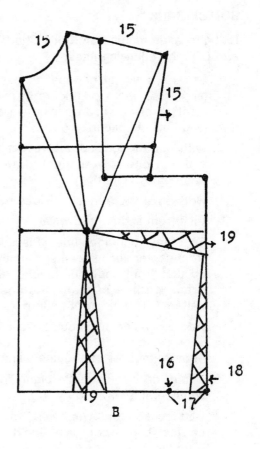

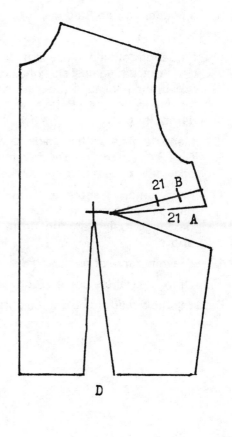

PATTERN IN THE ROUGH

BODICE BACK

Using measurements from Body Chart, DRAW and DOT the following lines:

0. Using a sheet of newspaper, cut a rectangle the width of underarm measurement (#5 on chart), divided by two, and the length of the paper.

1. With one straight edge of paper toward you and one to your right, draw center back (#1 on chart).

2. Horizontal line at neck, divided by two.

3. Line from shoulder to waist.

4. To obtain shoulder line: Place pattern front-center against center of back. Slide so that front shoulder touches dot #2. Trace outline of front shoulder onto pattern. Remove front pattern.

5. Add extension to shoulder to allow for shoulder dart, 1/2 to 1 inch, depending upon roundness of shoulders and neck.

6. Center neck to shoulder blade line, then shoulder line, divided by two.

7. Dart location for lower back. Draw in dart center from underarm line to waist. Approximate for now. Correct underarm line after you do Step #9.

8. Waist line.

9. For length of side, close side dart of pattern front. Lay against side of back pattern. Dot armhole location (also get correction for underarm line). Pattern will bulge at dart point (A).

10. Measure distance from side to waist dot. Give 3/4 inch to side. Divide remainder on each side of dart center.

11. Find center of shoulder. Draw shoulder dart-center, aiming at lower dart. Draw in dart legs, using amount from Step #5 above.

12. Draw in curve of neck.

13. Draw in armhole curve. Cut out pattern.

Pattern is now ready to be drafted onto muslin.

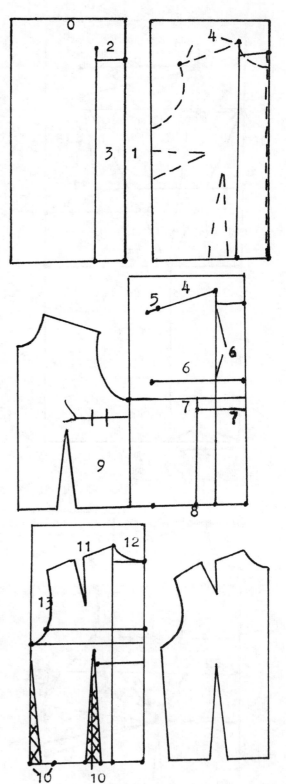

SKIRT BACK

Skirt back must be drafted before skirt front. Skirt back is also drafted upside down.

Draw and dot the following lines on paper:

1. With straight edge of paper to your left and straight edge toward you, measure across paper from left to right the measurement of the broadest part of your hip (#2 on chart). Dot.

2. A newspaper is about 23 inches long. Use as your skirt length. Fold paper at dot to form a rectangle. Cut off excess.

3. Waist will be toward you, center back to left. Measure from waist (#3 on chart) to broadest part of hip. Draw hip line.

4. Refer to E on measuring chart and dot 3 inches in on hip line.

5. Refer to F on measuring chart and draw this line from hip line to waist. Dot. Now make a dot 3 inches from waist on this line.

6. Refer to G on chart and draw this measurement at waist.

7. Refer to H on chart and draw this measurement 3 inches below waist.

8. Fill in side with curved line to form hip curve. Cut off excess.

9. Refer to D on chart and dot this measurement at center back. This is your hip curvature.

10. Draw a curved line to side. Cut off.

11. Take bodice back and place center to center skirt back.

12. Match inside dart leg of bodice to skirt. Dot skirt.

13. Line up side of bodice to side of skirt. Match bodice dart with skirt and dot. These dot positions are for your dart legs on skirt back. (If this dart measures over 2 inches at waist, you may give some of the control to the side waist and re-draw hip curve.)

14. Find center of dart legs and draw a straight line to lower hip line. *(cont'd next page)*

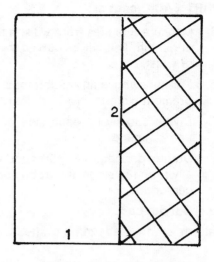

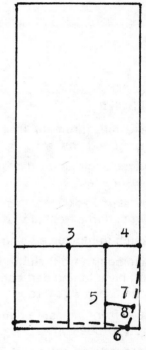

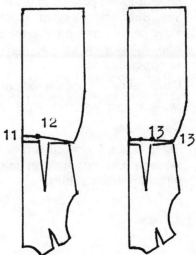

PATTERN IN THE ROUGH

SKIRT BACK (cont'd)

15. Measure 3 inches from waist and draw line for upper hip. This will be curved the same as curve of waist.

16. Measure above line. Subtract upper hip measurement from this (#1 on chart).

17. Divide equally on each side of dart center at upper hipline.

18. Draw in dart legs. Length of dart will form naturally from hip slope. It may be shorter than dart-center line.

19. Cut out dart.

Pattern is now ready to be drafted onto muslin.

SKIRT FRONT

1. Take measurement from #2 on measuring chart. Divide by two.

2. Cut rectangle as you did for skirt back using this measurement.

3. Lay skirt back onto this rectangle, matching skirt patterns from hip down.

4. Sketch in hip curve using skirt back as guide.

5. Take bodice front and repeat method used on skirt back to find dart control position for skirt front (Steps #11 through 14).

6. Take front measurement #1 on measuring chart. Divide by two.

7. Measure skirt pattern at 3 inches below waistline. Subtract above measurement from this. Your pattern may have same measurement as body measurement. If so, dart will extend only to upper hipline.

8. Divide equally on each side of dart center.

9. Draw in dart legs.

10. Cut out dart.

11. Draw in a 1/4-inch curvature at waist. This is average. You may have to adjust when you try on your muslin pattern.

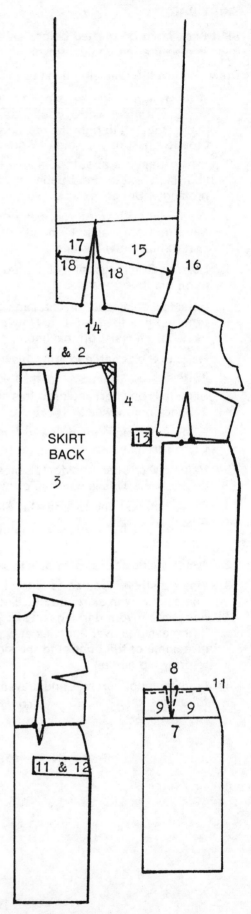

SLEEVE

1. Measure a paper rectangle the length of your arm (#7 on chart) and arm measurement (#2 on chart).

2. Divide pattern equally with a line.

3. Measure 5 to 6 inches from top of rectangle, depending upon figure size; 5-1/2 inches is average.

4. Draw line across pattern at the above measurement. This is the cap line.

5. Measure armhole of bodice front and back from drafted patterns. Note #5 below.

6. Measure curve of armholes.

7. Transfer measurements to cap line of pattern. Draw cap curves.

8. Draw top curve of sleeve.

9. Measure sleeve cap all around.

10. If measurement is 1 to 1-1/2 inches more than armhole (#3 above), perfect. If measurement is more, there will be too much ease. To correct, drop top of curve. Measure again.

11. Measure bottom of pattern and subtract wrist measurement (#5 on chart).

12. Divide this and give equal amount to each side.

13. Draw connecting lines between cap and wrist. Cut out pattern.

14. Draw elbow line (#6 on chart).

15. Slice this line from back side of pattern to within 1/4 inch of front of pattern.

16. Spread to give 1/2 inch elbow dart. You may use as dart or treat as ease.

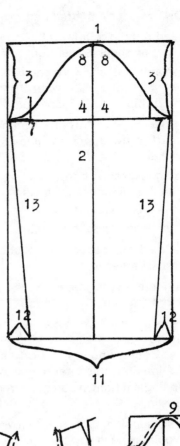

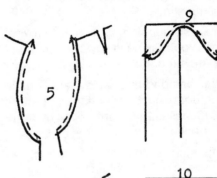

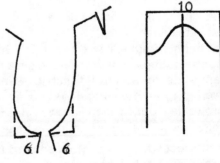

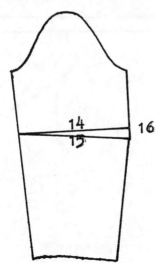

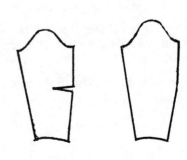

PATTERN IN THE ROUGH

PANT FRONT (Must be drafted before Pant Back)

You need only to rough-draft a pant pattern knee length to check for fit. The length of a newspaper sheet is just right.

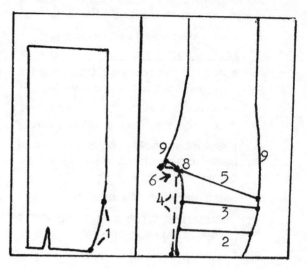

1. With straight edge toward you (which will be the waist) and using skirt front, trace outline of hip curve 6 inches onto paper.

2. Using measurement from #1 on measuring chart, draw upper hip line 3 inches below waist.

3. Using measurement from #2 on chart, draw hip line 6 inches from waist.

4. Using measurement from #3 on chart, draw line from waist to curvature.

5. Draw line from panty line to curvature using chart measurements.

6. If this line does not meet line #4 above, bring in #4 to meet panty line.

7. Draw line across from curvature line. This determines stride and should be 1-1/2 to 3 inches, depending upon body size. It should line up with center of inside leg. If you don't get it right, it can be corrected in the muslin.

8. Draw stride, sloping 1 inch below above line. You may need to correct center front at this time. Follow dots #2 and #3.

9. Draw inside and outside legs, curving as you do. Make bottom edge of pattern 9 to 10 inches at this point — can be corrected in muslin.

10. This step is one that I find most female figures need to obtain well-fitting pants. The hipline of the female figure has a tendency to cause pants to swing inward and not hang straight. To correct this, I have found a simple solution: just slice the panty line to within 1/4 inch of center. Overlap 1/2 inch (average). As you see, this **throws leg out.** It also throws waist up, which we will take care of in next step.

11. To correct waist, lay bottom edge of pattern against a straight surface. Cut off portion of waist that protrudes up.

12. Draw in waist dart by subtracting actual waist measurement from pattern measurement.

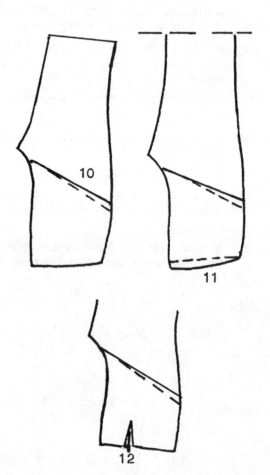

Pattern is now ready to be drafted onto muslin.

PANT BACK

1. Lay pattern front on newspaper, matching up bottom of front pattern with upper edge of newspaper. Secure with paper weights.

2. Trace outline of side front onto the newspaper.

3. Trace front stride curve and extend 3 inches beyond.

4. Remove pattern front.

5. Using skirt back, place hip-waist point against hip-waist point of above outline. Trace waistline onto pant pattern.

6. Trace dart from skirt onto pattern. Remove skirt pattern.

7. Draw in hipline 3 inches below waist using #1 on chart. This will be worked on either side of dart.

8. Draw hipline 6 inches below waist using #2 on chart. If dart extends below this line, work on either side of dart.

9. Find panty line from #3 on chart. Draw angling line to stride.

10. Measure front stride and subtract from total stride measurement.

11. Use this measurement to complete back stride. You may have to extend beyond what you have already drawn. Complete the center back from waist to stride using dots to guide you.

12. Draw inside leg — the straighter, the fuller the area under the seat will be.

13. Cut out pattern.

Pattern is now ready to be traced onto muslin.

NOTE: One of my students asked me to write that, no matter how funny the pant pattern looks, go ahead and make up into muslin. You'll be surprised how well it fits. Correct to perfection.

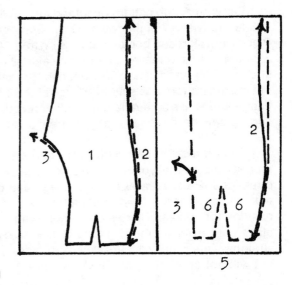

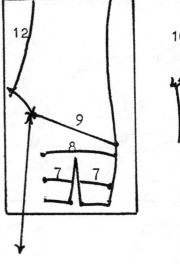

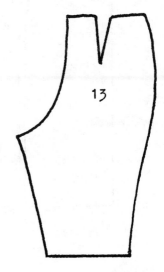

THE MUSLIN PATTERN

Lay your rough pattern on folded muslin or an old sheet that has been pressed and folded in half lengthwise. Weight down. Draw with pen or pencil very carefully around pattern outline. Place front skirt and bodice patterns on fold. Add 5/8-inch seams everywhere but armhole. Add 3/8-inch seams to these. Do not put seam allowance at neck but stay-stitch on edge to prevent stretch. Only short sleeves are needed for trial pattern. Cut about 4 inches below cap line. Cut out muslin pattern and sew with large stitch on your machine. It's best not to put a zipper in the back — just have someone pin muslin on you. Do leave sufficient space at back to get into. Be sure to sew on the lines that you drew to outline the pattern.

To complete muslin pattern for pants: Add 3/8-inch seams everywhere but waist. Add 1 inch at waist so that you will have extra to work with if stride is too short. Sew according to above directions. Press creases onto pant legs, using front dart as center of crease. NOTE: When you make a pair of pants from final pattern, you will match inside and outside leg seams to obtain position for crease. There's one other thing you should know about cutting out pants: Always place pant front on the fold side of the fabric. Sometimes fabric weave is off, or not woven straight. This usually occurs at selvage side. The off-weave will cause pant front to hang poorly but will not affect the pant back as much.

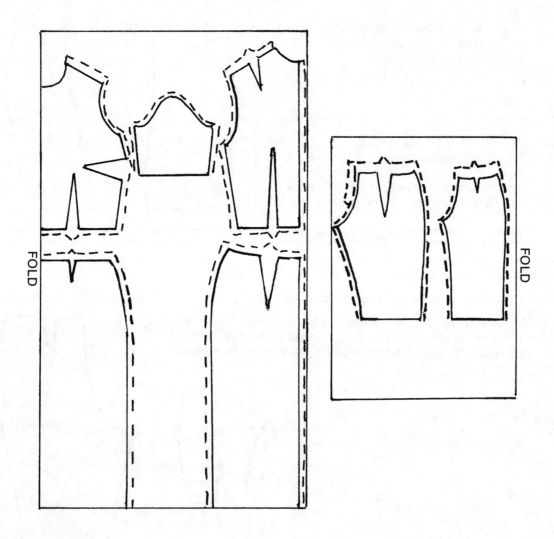

WORKING OUT THE BUGS — PANTS

Complete muslin as directions state at beginning of chapter.

Check for:

Look Down: Does crease aim toward center of shoe? If inward, give more control to hip (#10 on Pant Front, Pattern in the Rough).

Feel Pant Legs. If you can pick up excess at sides, pin it out.

Sit Down. Is crotch comfortable? Remember, you are using fabric with little stretch so make allowance. Knit will give more room.

TOO TIGHT AT STRIDE CURVATURE. ADD MORE. TOO MUCH AT FRONT OF LEG. PIN OUT. NOT ENOUGH ROOM FOR SEAT. ADD TO LEG.

Does stride area in back pucker on the seamline? This indicates the seam is too shallow. Scoop out, sew again and try on to see if corrected. Make necessary corrections on rough draft pattern and transfer to permanent pattern.

TO DRAW FINAL PATTERN:

Front: (1) Use yardstick to draw straight line across a piece of paper about 6 inches longer than pant length. (2) Draw a perpendicular line to above, the length of pant measurement (#6 on chart). (3) Lay corrected rough pattern front on line, centering leg. (4) Adjust so that each side of leg is even distance from bottom line. (5) Trace around pattern and add leg extension. See chapter on pants for flare leg. Cut out pattern.

Back: Lay cut-out pattern on another piece of paper. (6) Trace outline of outside leg and bottom edge. (7) Remove and place rough pattern back in outline with side of pattern touching outline drawing. There may be a slight difference in the line-up. If so, follow outline rather than side of pattern. Complete pattern by drawing around waistline, stride and inside leg, drawing leg to bottom of pattern. There will be a difference in the leg measurement at the bottom. The back leg is larger, anywhere from 1 to 2 inches, depending upon size of figure. Cut out pattern.

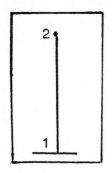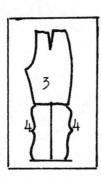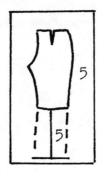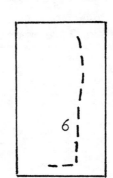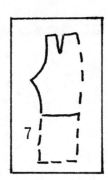

THE MUSLIN PATTERN

WORKING OUT THE BUGS — DRESS

Put on the muslin pattern and stand in front of a mirror. Does muslin lie smoothly over the body? If it does, you're lucky. More likely, there are a number of things to be corrected. Look for the following:

1. **Side Dart of Bodice Front:** Does it point toward bust or is it too high or too low? Draw correction on muslin. Make change on rough pattern as diagram on opposite page shows.

2. **Shoulder Line:** Does it divide body properly, or is it too far to the back or front? Draw correction on muslin. Make change on rough pattern.

3. **Back of Neck:** Is it loose? Pin darts on muslin at neckline. Make correction on rough pattern by enlarging shoulder dart. This pulls the neck in for smooth fit.

4. **Back Bodice at Armhole:** Is area loose? Pin tuck in muslin. Make correction on rough pattern by slicing from armhole to shoulder dart and overlapping. This makes shoulder dart larger, which gives needed shaping.

5. **Put a String Around Natural Waistline:** Does the waistline of the muslin fall under the string? If so, perfect. But if it falls above or below, make corrections as follows: If muslin waistline is too high, rip out seam and pull skirt to proper position. Measure space left between skirt and bodice. Apply to rough pattern. If waistline of muslin is too long, there will be looseness around the ribcage. Pin tuck at ribcage of muslin. Correct on rough pattern by taking off bottom of bodice. Apply same to bodice back.

6. **Bubble on Sleeves at Armhole:** Bodice front or back at chest line is too narrow, or shoulder may be too short. Generally, when shoulders are too short, the sleeves will pull up on the outside. Make correction on rough pattern by adding to the chest line, shoulder or both.

7. **Pulled Look Across Upper Chest:** Indicates pattern is too small at this area. Make correction on rough pattern by adding to armhole. Take off pattern if there is overall looseness at this area.

8. **Looseness at Neckline:** Neckline is too wide. Correct pattern as diagram shows.

9. **Skirt Hiked in Front:** Add to top of skirt pattern.

10. **Skirt Hangs in Front:** Take off top of skirt pattern.

11. **Loose Play Over Area Above Derriere:** Make more slope at waist of pattern skirt back.

12. **Bubbles at Hipline:** Pin muslin to smooth out. Take this amount off pattern.

There may be other things to correct. Remember: whatever you do to correct the muslin, apply same to rough pattern. Take off or add to where needed. Good luck!

WORKING OUT THE BUGS

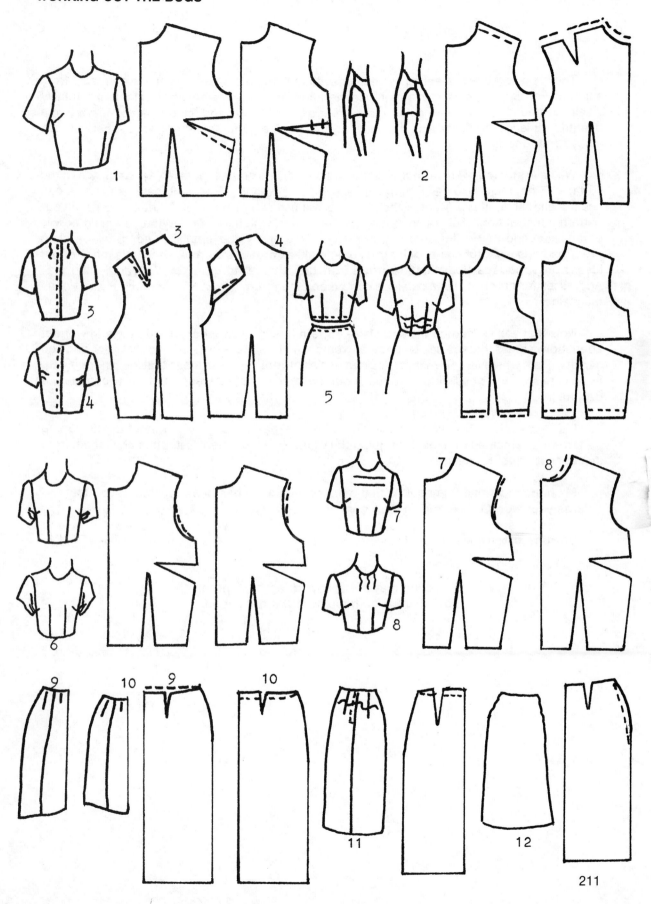

THIS IS IT!

There's a very special feeling connected with looking at something you have created from scratch. Perhaps it comes from our pioneer heritage, or maybe it's inborn. But there's definitely a self-satisfaction from being able to take a flat piece of fabric and, step by step, turn it into a beautiful finished product. And it's knowing that you've done something today that you can enjoy for a long time.

We have studied over two-hundred design cuts in this course, but we've just scratched the surface. From these, you can *expand and expand and expand*. The combinations that you can use are almost limitless. Most of the time you will use two or more of the design cuts in your pattern construction. But you've gotten the basis with which to work. What you need now is enthusiasm and the feeling that you *can* do it. One of my star pupils, Sandy Sheldon (who proofread this work for clarity of instructions) makes gorgeous clothes. She gets many of her ideas from various catalogs that she orders from department stores in New York and California. Addresses for ordering these catalogs can be obtained from ads in *Harper's Bazaar* and *Vogue* magazines.

Now that you've learned the secrets of Pattern Design, no longer will you have to wonder about how a dress that you see on another woman or in a store is created. You'll know, and you can duplicate whatever you wish, or you can use all of your very own ideas that keep popping up in your head. And you'll find that your confidence will increase each time you complete a design.

It's been exciting to write this book. The pleasure that I have come to know from designing patterns has remained with me throughout the years. Every garment is another challenge, from its conception to its fruition.

My hope in writing this book is that a spark of interest has been created in you that will enlarge your world by expanding your concepts.

So don't just sit there! Go to it. *This is it!* This is the chance to use your talents! HAVE FUN.

"Action may not always bring happiness;
but there is no happiness without action."
. . . Disraeli